Keith

S.E.T. FOR
SUCCESS

(Structure, Engage, Transform)

A Roadmap to Transform Your Business

IT'S BEEN AWHILE. I HOPE YOU ARE WELL AND BUSINESS IS GREAT. YOU ARE HOLDING MY LIFE'S WORK IN YOUR HANDS. TREAT IT WELL.

Be Your Best,
INVEST IN THE SUCCESS OF OTHERS,
MAKE YOUR JOURNEY COUNT.

By Richard Lannon

Best Wishes

Richard. 2016

S.E.T. for Success - A Roadmap to Transform Your Business

First Printing 2015

Publish by BraveWorld Publishing
braveworld.ca/

Library and Archives Canada Cataloguing in Publications

Lannon, Richard A., 1962-

S.E.T. for Success: A Roadmap to Transform Your Business was written by Richard Lannon; diagrams and illustrations by Richard Lannon and ShahMaeen Orakzai , primary editor Usnea Lebendig, secondary editor Annie Daylon, proofreading by David Day, Rob Wozny, John Hindle and Jeannette Lannon, book cover and interior designed by Sel P.

ISBN 978-0-9938697-0-9

1. Strategic Planning 2. Business Analysis 3. Leadership Development 4. Business Roadmap

Printed and bound in Canada

For inquiries and bulk orders please contact info@braveworld.ca

Praise for S.E.T. for Success

"You owe it to yourself to not just read S.E.T. for Success, but to apply this business roadmap to realize your objectives. It is a beautifully written book that will challenge and inspire you. Are you struggling with an approach for getting started on your strategic planning efforts? If so, Richard Lannon has written a masterpiece of wise counsel for you. This book is for anyone in pursuit of excellence in strategic planning. It is time to change, grow, and be S.E.T. for Success!"

– Steve Gilliland, author,
Enjoy the Ride, International Speaker
....

"In *S.E.T. for Success*, Richard Lannon offers actionable steps for anyone in business who find themselves stuck, having lost focus, or lacking direction. Being intimately familiar with all three of those realities at different times in my career, I particularly appreciate the clarity and very real world assistance that Richard provides. This isn't just an 'interesting' business book - this is a book that you'll USE to take your business to the next level."

– Joe Calloway, author,
Magnetic: The Art Of Attracting Business
....

"In his book, S.E.T. for Success, Richard Lannon takes the reader from the carefully-designed planning stage to action roadmap using a proven model that addresses key business impact zones. By using many business and personal examples, you'll learn exactly what is needed and why it is important. Get ready to bridge the gap from the strategic to the tactical through creation of your roadmap that enables you to forge your journey of business success. Please, read this book. Your success depends on it!"

– Adam Witty,
Advantage Media Group, Founder and CEO
••••••••••••••••••••••••••••••

"S.E.T. for Success is a great resource for any business or organization that needs to get their bearings and headings. Not only does Lannon make the case for strategic planning, he provides the motivation and the step-by-step guide in this book. More than just another book on strategy, this work can help transform your business for tomorrow's challenges. This book provides a much-needed roadmap from idea inception through implementation. All the fluff is gone and this book is packed with usable, real-world ideas. Before you engage in strategic planning, read and implement this book. You'll be glad you did."

– Terry Brock, syndicated columnist,
professional speaker, marketing coach
••••••••••••••••••••••••••••••

"SET for success is a clearly written, systematic proven system for business leaders to create their own implementable plan/ blueprint to guide and create a successful future. I recommend it."

– Brian Lee, CSP, Founder and CEO,
Custom Learning Systems Group Ltd.
••••••••••••••••••••••••••••••

"Peter Drucker said, "Culture eats strategy for breakfast". S.E.T. for Success brings clarity to strategic planning by providing a roadmap on how to engage your people and culture at every step of the planning process with clear measures. An organization cannot plan in a vacuum without involving the people who will make it happen."

– Bob Parker, CSP, Author & Facilitator,
The Pit Crew Challenge: Winning Customers
Through Teaming

....

"Richard Lannon has decades of experience in business development and growth. He has worked in a wide variety of organisations and business fields. He is a proven entrepreneur. He has studied business and operated business's for many years. What you are about to receive as you engage with this material is well proven, authentic and successful business practices. We had the opportunity to host one of his Seminars in the UK. The reception was outstanding for the seasoned business owner and for the new to the world of commercial development. I am confident this will be a great addition to our intercellular capital to build a successful business enterprise."

– Ian Green,
Executive Director, Proton Foundation

....

"All of my success in business came from practicing models of success - that's what you get in spades in SET for Success. Read it and succeed."

– Hugh Culver,
author, Give Me A Break-the art of making time work for you

....

"Knowing what is important in business is one thing. Being able to implement is another. In S.E.T. for Success, Richard Lannon guides you through the process of identifying those initiatives that you must focus on and helps you craft a business roadmap that you can implement to drive your success. The book presents great real business stories, examples and outcomes. A must read!"

– Stephanie Staples,
Your Life Unlimited, Author, When Enlightening Strikes.

....

"Richard Lannon has been in the business trenches and speaks and writes from experience. Many years as a consultant have given him a broad background to draw from. His ability to understand business systems and see strengths and weaknesses is powerful for any business. If you want your business to maximize its potential, this book is one you need to read. I wish I had read it years ago!"

– John Hindle, Entrepreneur,
Former GM Winnipeg Goldeyes

....

"My friend Richard Lannon has been helping entrepreneurs and professionals set solid foundations for success and strategic growth for many years. His 'SET for Success' needs to be in every business owner's library. Actually, it needs to be well read, studied to be understood, and applied if they want to see their teams and their enterprise succeed. 'SET for Success' can be a strategic investment in your future – but you have to act on it."

– Bob 'Idea Man' Hooey,
author 'Legacy of Leadership' and 'Make ME Feel Special!'
www.ideaman.net

....

"This book shows you how to become absolutely clear about your values, vision, mission, purpose and goals, and exactly what you need to do to increase your sales and profitability immediately."

– Brian Tracy, author, *The Road to Wealth*

....

Dedication

To My Life Line

To Jeannette, Matthew and Alexander:
"You are everything to me."

Acknowledgement

In my mind this book has taken longer to write than it should have. When asked, I say it really took more than 10 years to create—only a year and eight months to write and publish. The other years were the forming years.

With that in mind I want to thank all the people who tolerated me during the journey of writing this book. As with most writers, I started talking about the writing of this book long before I actually wrote it.

The following individuals deserve special thanks.

My wife Jeannette was a sounding board for ideas and listened to me as I continually spouted off all the virtues of the S.E.T. process and SET-Ability model. There must have been many, many times that she rolled her eyes and thought, write the book already. I'm grateful for her tolerance.

Patty Moore (Mount Royal University), who years ago encouraged me to write a book related to business analysis, strategic planning and road map development. She's been an inspiration to me for years and I wish her the best that life can bring. She really wanted to see me succeed far beyond being a university professor and instructor. Her thoughts during the early years of the development of the business analysis program paid off. Now I get to thank her for all her insight, feedback, encouragement and success.

My writing coach, Les Kletke, for his insight and guidance through the writing process that helped get this book to draft format. To my content editor, Usnea Lebendig, for her work on the content and copy editing of this book. I am sure when she looked at the first draft of the book she realized that it needed a lot of work. She encouraged me and taught me some valuable lessons about writing, communications and business content driven endeavours that benefit the audience, the reader. Annie Daylon, author, for her review and edits of the book. She assisted in tightening things up and making additional suggestions that were incorporated.

And finally, I'd like to acknowledge all of the great people at great companies I've worked with over the course of my career, and all the students I've taught. In a very special way you helped me discover and apply the process discussed in this book.

Special Acknowledgements:

To the business leaders, professionals and peers who relentlessly encouraged me to get this book done. You have been a good thorn in my side: Hugh Culver, Annie Daylon, John Hindle, Stephanie Staples, Derek Johannson, Rob Wozny, Dorothy Lannon, and David Day. I am sure I drove each one of these people a little nuts with my questions. Thanks for being there for me.

Finally, my nieces, Andrea and Dorothy Eggenberger, for being the 'twenty somethings' who provided insight and thought for a younger more hip generation. It was great to find a way to include you in my business writing endeavours. Thank you for that privilege.

Table of Contents

Part 1: Be S.E.T. for Success in Your Business 1

    Introduction..3

    The SET-Ability Model Revealed 12

Part 2: Setting the Ground Work............................25

    Question Your Business 27

    Stakeholders have Business Impact 38

Part 3: Know Where You Want to Go 53

    Vision and Mission for the Future 55

    Values and Guiding Principles.............................68

    Goals and Objectives 80

Part 4: Focus on Your Key Business Impact Zones.............89

    Process and Productivity......................................91

    Tools and Technology 103

    Business Development..113

    People and Culture...127

    Measurements and the Financials......................141

Part 5: Plan It - Map It - Implement It! Go the Distance. 153

The Strategic Map 155

The Actionable Roadmap 170

The Work Plan... 182

Communication Plan and Map............................. 193

Go the Distance! 203

PART ONE

Be S.E.T. for Success in Your Business

Structure, Engage, Transform

*"Start with an approach and apply a model to
start your journey well"*
– Richard Lannon

1
Introduction

"Twenty years from now you will be more disappointed by the things that you didn't do than by the ones you did do. So throw off the bowlines. Sail away from the safe harbor. Catch the trade winds in your sails. Explore. Dream. Discover."
– Mark Twain

Are You S.E.T. for Success in Your Business?

Every business leader has a winding road they travel on, a road filled with uncertainty, challenging decisions, and the increasing need to keep up with the breakneck speed of change in their field, their industry, and the world around them. They know the road to their success is fraught with peaks, valleys and detours, all of which need to be skillfully navigated. Yet even the best business leaders can get stuck sometimes, causing them to lose their focus and need to re-establish direction. When this happens they often find they need a new plan, an approach that will help them to get to where they need to go—a roadmap, if you will.

A roadmap points the business in its best direction, displaying important linkages and intersections, and bringing it most effectively and efficiently to its end goal. To keep from getting stuck (and also to get unstuck) , a business needs a navigational tool that maps boundaries and points of interest, displaying business development opportunities, process efficiencies, tools that can be used, and the people that can make the successful journey happen, all right in front of their eyes. This is where strategic planning comes in.

Strategic planning is a systematic process of envisioning a desired future, translating this vision into broadly defined goals or objectives, and then mapping out a concrete sequence of steps to achieve them. Unlike long-term planning, which begins with the current status and lays down a path to meet estimated future needs , **strategic planning begins with the desired end and works backward to the current status.**[1] Rather than focusing on internal operational "issues," a strategic focus addresses and solves business problems and opportunities from a larger, over-arching scope of focus. It's formulated before tactical action is taken.

To be truly successful in your business, you and your teams need to not only engage in strategic planning, but also do so using a structured approach that identifies your business challenges and opportunities, establishes your key priorities, and builds a roadmap with action items that can be directly implemented by your team. The S.E.T. approach and the SET-Ability model outlined in chapter two of this book is one of those proven approaches that will help you map out your journey so you can achieve long term business success.

Peaks, Valleys and Detours

I am privileged to be able to meet with business leaders, their teams and professionals. I regularly hear about the peaks, valleys and the detours (otherwise known as the good, the bad and the unexpected) that take place on the road to success. Whatever the stories, the top three things business leaders and their teams say when they experience challenges are: I'm stuck; I've lost focus; I lack direction.

I'm Stuck

A business leader in the healthcare industry recently confided that they felt stuck in their business. The metaphor they described was being trapped in a box with all the flaps tightly closed and no way out. They then paused and said they'd never expressed it that way before and that the honesty felt good. It was a moment of truth.

Feeling stuck in your business is not unusual, especially when there is so much going on—so many decisions to be made. It's normal. Sometimes a business has too much opportunity or not enough. Perhaps your company is experiencing rapid growth and things are changing too quickly, or maybe you are over extended with too much risk. Maybe your personnel turnover is too high. Or the external market has changed around you. You could even be suffering from poor leadership, management or resource capabilities.

The important thing is what you do about it—how you move forward, the actions you take to get unstuck. The key is to look at the sense of being stuck as a business opportunity.

I've Lost Focus

Another thing that often happens when challenges set in is that we lose our focus. It happens to the best of us. From the time we're kids and into adulthood we're told we need to focus if we want to be successful, but we're rarely told what "to focus" actually means or how to achieve it. I believe that it isn't until we lose something of importance that we truly understand what focus means. That is a powerful insight.

I was asked to facilitate a strategic planning process for a company in the transportation industry over a six month period. My job was to help them understand what they needed to focus on for their business to reach the next level. As part of that process I always do pre-work, which in this case was having one-to-one private meetings with the senior management team and the company representatives.

In one such meeting, the president revealed that his company had just lost a large contract, one that amounted to nearly a third of their revenue. What's more, he didn't know why. He felt as if he'd really lost focus in his business. The state of having a clear visual definition of his business was missing, and he hadn't been paying enough attention to the core of his business and that client in particular. He'd taken the contract for granted and allowed himself and his team to get distracted by other things when they should have been focusing on ensuring that one of their largest accounts was maintained and grown. That loss really shook the company. They weren't sure what they were going to do, how to make up this major loss.

I Lack Direction

Another client, an oil and gas service company, had experienced rapid growth. They'd started out in the president's home and ten years later they numbered over 150 people. That is some serious growth! Their expansion happened so quickly, in fact, that they'd had no time to standardize their processes. People felt as if they were tripping over one another and no one was clear where the business was going. So much opportunity happening so fast resulted in creating an unstable business environment and a lack of clarity. They needed a direction.

As the president and I worked together, we decided to engage a representative team from the organization to help identify the issues and find ways to rectify their challenges. We used an approach that provided clear boundaries, one that created a clear picture of their present situation and their preferred future state. This, in turn, provided much needed clarity. Afterwards, the team was able to identify that which they could realistically do to make concrete improvements in their organization. An action plan was developed to help the organization make the adjustments needed to move forward.

My dad, a successful entrepreneur, used to tell me when I was a boy, whatever you can conceive you can achieve. **If you can see it in your mind, you can make it happen.** Clarity is determining exactly what results you want to achieve, when you want to achieve them, and taking action to make it happen.

Why S.E.T. for Success

Truth be told, many organizations miss the chance to solve their business problems or leverage opportunities. Sometimes it's just a matter of not making time for the decision-making process or not having a common approach to help you figure things out. Making time for decision-making processes is a challenging issue. There's just so much going on—time is a limited resource. Yet if you don't make time for long-term decision-making and planning, your challenges will continue to grow and worsen. You'll start to have problems with your processes, tools, sales and people within your organization. Your business leadership will end up spending more time, money and/or resources dealing with issues and putting out fires rather than moving coherently towards your strategic goals.

To prevent this, you need to apply a consistent approach, one that focuses on your business requirements and stakeholder needs. This is where the S.E.T. Approach comes in. The **S.E.T.** approach can be broken down into the following:

1. **Structure** your approach to understand your business
2. **Engage** your people to work together successfully and make better decisions
3. **Transform** your business through establishing a common direction

This is the approach I've used over the past 10 years in working with clients to help them achieve the success they're looking for. Whether it's been a strategic planning session where we needed to develop a strategy map and action roadmap with clear milestones, a business and executive coaching session with a focus on building the business capabilities of a senior professional, or helping a team focus on a specific business requirement like business development opportunities or process and productivity improvements, the S.E.T. Approach has been successfully applied to all sorts of business situations.

Structure Your Approach: The best way to begin to understand your business problems and opportunities is through a structured analysis. This often involves a combination of interviews, questionnaires and assessments to get some benchmarks of where your business and its processes currently stand.

Engage Your People: Your people are one of your greatest assets. It's important to harness their knowledge and get them engaged in helping you understand your business and its challenges. This is often done through group meetings and facilitated workshops. The key is to let your people help you unravel complex issues and make key decisions.

Transform Your Business: There are many aspects of transformation planning. In this case I'm referring to creating an actionable roadmap, work-plans and communication plans for your business environment. Whatever it takes for you and your people to actually take action and create change.

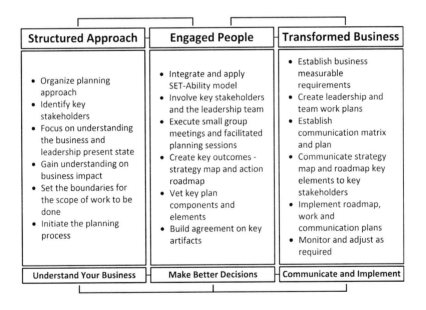

Figure 1-1: The Three Step S.E.T. Approach to Planning

Past, Present, Future

Planning is an exercise in gathering and documenting information about the past, present and future of your business. It has to do with understanding the needs of your business, stakeholders, solutions and transitions. Documenting your past, present and future will help you determine where you want to go over the next few years, how you're going to get there, and how to recognize when you've arrived.

A Candid Look

From time to time to time you'll need to take a candid look at your business. This candid look is essential to understanding the reasons *why* you're stuck, are having a hard time finding your focus, and/or have lost your direction. Keep in mind though, this hard, honest look can be particularly challenging. Every business leader I've ever interviewed has, from time to time, felt extraordinary pain in being honest about their business.

Yet having self-awareness is one of the most important qualities of great business leadership and is foundational for good planning. To be honest means that you are willing to look at your strengths and weaknesses and to find ways to address issues, even if doing so is painful. This willingness will make you a better business leader.

Build Plans with Deliverables

A deliverable is something that is produced as the result of a project and delivered to customers, either internal or external. It can be tangible (i.e. a physical product) or intangible (i.e. a service). A good planning approach will yield concrete deliverables and clear outcomes.

An outcome is a positive change that results from a successful planning process. Every organization can benefit from some common deliverables using an approach that can help them clarify and achieve their outcomes. Some of the outcomes you should expect from the S.E.T. approach include:

- Apply a systematic approach to strategic planning and implementation
- Create a strategy map outlining key business focus areas
- Establish leading and lagging indicators for your success measurements
- Build an implementation roadmap to guide your future success
- Create a communication matrix for your plan implementation
- Enhance team commitment to the things you must get done

Final Thoughts

No matter where you are in your business or in what way you plan to move forward, it is important that you have an approach to follow. This will help you add discipline to your planning endeavours and make it easier for you and your people to successfully follow through. With the right approach and model in place, you'll find your leadership team able to make much better business decisions, your business able to move forward, and your people able to produce concrete, measureable results.

This book will outline in detail how you can structure your approach, engage your people and transform your business through using the S.E.T. Approach and the SET-Ability model as a way to improve your business, both today and in the future.

2

The SET-Ability Model Revealed

Challenge is the pathway to engagement and progress in our lives. But not all challenges are created equal. Some challenges make us feel alive, engaged, connected, and fulfilled. Others simply overwhelm us. Knowing the difference as you set bigger and bolder challenges for yourself is critical to your sanity, success, and satisfaction.

– Brendon Burchard

Want to Succeed More in Business?
Use a Model to Put it all Together!

One way to get your business back on track is to use a model with clear parameters and guidelines. My model is the "SET-Ability" model. By my definition, the word 'SET-Ability' refers to the ability to fine-tune your business to achieve consistent, measurable results for positive business impact.

There are a number of factors that you can set within your business that will alter its performance in key business impact zones – business development, process and productivity, tools and technology and people and culture. Fine-tuning these impact zones will allow your business to work more efficiently and effectively, allowing you to get the best out of each different part of your business as well as the company as a whole.

What's more, the SET-Ability model can be used at the strategic, tactical or operational level of planning for your business.

Technical Connection

Strictly defined, SET-Ability refers to the fine-tuning of technical instruments and the parameters one needs to pay attention to in order to get the greatest functionality out of a piece of technology. In fact, many of the parameters used to fine-tune items such as your television, radio, and car can also be successfully applied to the business thinking of a professional, team or organization. The intended results for business (as well as the instruments!) are optimized functioning, followed by long term impact and success.

Application to Your Business

The world around us is filled with things that have settings. Whether we're talking about current technology (your smart phone, for example) or the mechanical inventions of the past, if the working parameters of the item aren't set correctly, it will not operate at their highest capacity. Some won't even work at all.

Fine Tuning a Television

From the dawn of the television era, TV sets required fine tuning. With the old televisions, viewers would sometimes have to move their television to just the right place in the house to get a solid picture. Other strategies included jiggling the antennas and/or adding tinfoil to the tips in order to get a decent picture.

These televisions even had vertical and horizontal hold buttons that would have to be adjusted each time one wanted to catch a show. Can you imagine standing there turning knobs to get your picture right? (There were no remote controls.) There was always some sort of line across the screen or a slight buzz in the volume as Bobby scored in the good old hockey game, as the Fonz said, "Ayyyyyyyyy" on *Happy Days,* or as you watched the first landing on the moon. Imagine having these issues today, on your smart television, while watching the Super Bowl, the news, your favourite Star Wars movie or as Barney Stinson said, *"It's gonna be legen — wait for it — dary." on How I Met Your Mom,* or *on some other show you like. Really.*[2]

Eventually, televisions evolved from tubes to transistors to flat screens and things improved. Even with technology today, you have to fine-tune your television to get the most out of it. Smart televisions require a certain amount of configuration when you install them, and although some of that configuration is automatic, we all still play with the settings to get them right.

Sometimes while you are binge watching your favourite Netflix's show, your smart television and surround sound system go out of alignment: the picture and audio are out of sync. So you use the remote, press settings, audio and automatic alignment and, just like that, the problem is solved. The technology parameters had to be re-set for the alignment of the smart television and audio so it functioned properly together again. And like televisions, a business has to work within certain parameters and to be aligned. If it doesn't, it will not work correctly.

That's the SET-Ability factor.

Smart Devices Are Not So Smart

There are many other items that require fine-tuning. Some are self-correcting, adjusting themselves automatically based on the parameters of the hardware and the software they're running (i.e. computers, phones or smart devices). However, if a new piece of software is installed incorrectly, is corrupted, or if the hardware is defective, operational conflicts will occur, perhaps causing the entire system to cease operating properly. Remember the last time you upgraded your computer's software and forgot to check the compatibility with one of your favourite programs and it stopped working? The same happens in business all the time.

Compromising Your Business

Recently one of the Android smart phone companies released a new operating system for their phones. The outcome was that the phones froze, batteries died faster, and a number of applications did not work. As you can imagine, the customer base was not happy! What was once the number one phone company became compromised as customers complained and, finding no solution, began looking for alternative products to buy.

Android had rushed its Operating Systems (OS) deployment without fully working out all of the bugs. In doing so, they also managed to break a contract, the agreement that things would work. Put another way, the operating system didn't work within the agreed upon parameters. The result? The consumers' interest shifted.

As you are probably well aware, today's customers have little tolerance for error. This company missed the opportunity to maintain or improve on the way their customers expected them to operate – they provided a bad technology and the customer's faith and satisfaction declined. They made some bad decisions that had negative consequences, and those decisions rippled around the world at the click of a button.

Taking a Ride in Your Car

Another example of SET-Ability can be seen in automobiles: your car, van, or truck--whatever you drive. Think about it from a customer perspective. Customers have needs and desires which need to be met when it comes to the purchase and use of an automobile. Regardless of your vehicle's shape, size or colour, every automobile is a machine that has to operate within certain parameters and on a consistent basis.

For example, automotive electronics are used to control the engine. The motor must be in tune to run smoothly. The braking systems need to allow the vehicle to stop within a certain distance when the brakes are applied. When we say consistent basis, 99.9 percent of the time is not good enough. People expect their vehicles to operate properly, just like they expect your business to operate properly against a set of parameters that they created. Not you.

From customers to employees, from teams to business leaders, and even as an entire organization, there is always a SET-Ability factor. It's your ability to fine-tune your business so you can achieve consistent, measureable results that positively impact your business. It's no different than a television set, a computer or your automobile.

The SET-Ability Model

For the same reason we monitor and adjust equipment, all organizations also need to be adjusted to operate within the parameters that will get them to their highest level of functioning. So how to apply this to your business? To understand your SET-Ability factor we need to break down the SET-Ability model into its various components as identified in the diagram provided.

The SET-Ability model as a whole is made up of impact zones, ripple effects and outcomes. You cannot push on one without impacting the others. For example, if we push on business development, it will ripple out into the other impact zones. Add additional clients and there is pressure on your business processes, the tools you use and the people and culture of your organization. Say that something needs to be done more quickly, and you create an acceleration effect. If you adjust how your work gets done with your people and company culture, you will impact process and productivity, and so on. It is like the stone thrown into a pond: one stone, one ripple; multiple stones, multiple colliding ripples and major business impact.

As you can see in the SET-Ability Diagram in Figure 2-1, the model is broken down into key impact zones:

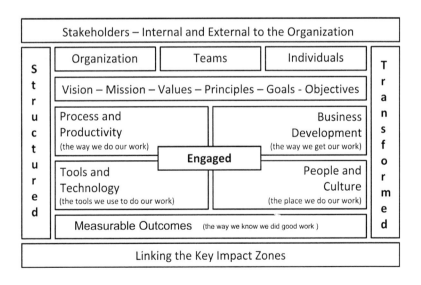

Figure 2-1: The SET-Ability Model Diagram for Planning

SET-Ability Business Impact Zones:

- **Stakeholders:** Every business has both internal and external stakeholders, as well as positive and negative stakeholders. These can include investors, government agencies, competitors and/or employees. Understanding stakeholders and their impact on a business is an area where a lot of businesses miss the mark.

- **Organization, Teams and Individuals:** Like a sports team, if these are working together well, then the business has a chance to be a champion. The idea is that everyone needs to be aligned to the common interests of the business.

- **Vision and Mission:** Every business needs to have a vision and mission. Vision embraces the future success of your business. Mission clearly states what you are all about. This is an area which a lot of business leaders and their teams (and therefore their employees!) misunderstand, thinking it is merely fluff. If this is true of your organization, it can cause serious problems in alignment, purpose, and your overall success factor.

- **Values and Guiding Principles:** True values are the core on which you build your company. Guiding principles are statements used to make business decisions.

- **Goals and Objectives:** These are the things you want to achieve. Goals are overarching, while objectives are specific. Goals and objectives can be written and translated at the three main levels within your company – the strategic, tactical and operational.

- **Process and Productivity:** This simply means the way we do our work. People complicate work processes and productivity-thinking all the time. This area is all about unraveling those complications and creating maximum efficiency and effectiveness.

- **Tools and Technology:** Simply put, these are whatever we use to do our work. That can mean a tractor, car, computer or even a pen. Changes in tools and technology can create major impacts on your business.

- **Business Development:** The way we get our work. Whether you are a profit or non-profit organization, we all engage in the art of business development in order to stay afloat and keep wind in our sails.

- **People and Culture:** This is a combination of both the place we work and the resources we use to get our work done. It is another of the most often underestimated areas of impact.

- **Measurement:** Understanding the common indicators that help guide business decisions. It is a matter of knowing the key measurements for your business and making sure you have the right indicators dialled in.

SET-Ability Model Methodology

The SET-Ability model comes into play once you and your team are ready to move to the planning and analysis level. In order to become a better business, make key decisions successfully, and have all of the key components of your business working well together, you and your team need to take a candid look at where you are and where it is you want to go. You then need to develop a plan of action detailing how to get there. The SET-Ability model methodology helps focus your thinking and clarifies what needs to be looked at and modified. It then provides you with a straightforward guide to follow.

One of the most important factors in improvement—one that you yourself need to bring to the table—is a burning desire to get where you want to go. There must be a recognition that something needs to be done, that the business can always be taken to the next level. And it's the business leader and management teams that are the ones to do it. You and your team must be prepared to do whatever it takes, even change your entire business environment, if needed.

Once you're ready to take your business to the next level, you can use the SET-Ability model for planning at various levels in the organization. These include:

- **Business Analysis:** an approach to understanding your business through identifying its needs and determining solutions to problems/opportunities. Solutions often include systems development, process improvement, organizational change, strategic planning and/or policy development.[3]

- **Enterprise Analysis:** connected to a part of business analysis, but similar in scope to portfolio management. The outcomes are usually a set of projects that go into the project portfolio, complete with business case support. They are ready for senior management to examine, choose and act on.[4]

- **Strategic Planning:** defining your business's strategy (or direction) and making decisions on allocating resources specifically to pursue this strategy.[5]

- **Program Planning:** a plan of action aimed at accomplishing a clear business objective, complete with details on what work is to be done, by whom, when, and what means or resources will be used to accomplish it.[6]

- **Project Planning:** relates to the use of schedules to plan and report progress within the project environment.[7]

- **Operational Planning**: the process of linking strategic goals and objectives to tactical and operational goals and objectives. It describes milestones and conditions for success, and explains how, or what portion of, a strategic plan will be put into operation during a given operational period.[8]

Like machines, organizations have many moving parts and all of the parts must be taken into consideration when making changes. Careful consideration must be given to each of the key business impact zones and the ripple effects that will be created when these are adjusted. The SET-Ability model, when considered in its entirety, allows you and your team to work through and fine-tune all of the different moving parts in your business. It becomes your opportunity to connect the dots, allowing the components of your organization to work better together and maximize their potential.

The Fine-tuned Business Machine

Think of your business as an advanced machine or technology with many moving parts that are always changing due to key environmental factors and its human elements. How would you fine-tune this machine and engage your resources to achieve its highest functioning?

Turning your business into a slick operating machine can significantly revolutionize your working environment. Consider what this really means. What if your people were all rowing in the same direction, in tune and with clear focus? How much more quickly (and even joyfully) your business would get to where you were going!

But how does one align all of these many moving parts, parts that are always changing? That's where the SET-Ability model comes into play. The SET-Ability model is useful for organizations that need to fine-tune their strategies or find out why what they're doing isn't working. An organization might also choose this model if it's experiencing a high amount of internal inefficiencies within a specific business impact zone.

If we use technical documents as a reference, words like resolution, parameters, amplitude, frequency and reliability would be used to describe the boundaries around operations. These are all great words and can easily be applied to business thinking. A deeper look into these words reveals an interesting business perspective:

> **Resolution:** This is your degree of sharpness and your determination to act upon something that you've decided to do. You do it with resolve. It is never too late to fine-tune your resolution or to re-make a decision on a change or a course of action. Consider writing down what it is you want to do and create the determination to make it happen. Just do it!

> **Parameters:** This is a variable that must have a specific value during the execution of a procedure. It usually has limits, boundaries or guidelines (i.e. an organizational policy or process, etc.). Like a technological setting, we all have parameters that we live by within our professional lives. As business leaders you should know the parameters by which you and the business operate. What's more, you need to make sure that your processes and people work within these very same business parameters.

Amplitude: This refers to greatness of size. It is the magnitude, the fullness, the breadth, or degree of change caused by sound waves. How loud are you expressing what it is you're wanting or willing to do? If you want to be successful, tell someone. Express your greatness, the magnitude and range that you are willing to go to. Figure out your greatness and grow your amplitude.

Frequency: This is the rate of occurrence, as in the number of periods or regularly occurring events of any given unit of time. How often do you do what you do? What is your consistency level? In order to achieve your resolution within the parameters that are set and within the amplitude you have expressed, what is the desired frequency? Frequency is important to your success. You must practice frequency of engaged and focused positive actions every single day.

Reliability: By definition, reliability is the extent to which a system or human element can be relied upon. This measure can relate to achievement, accuracy and/ or honesty. Reliability centers in trust. In a systems world, reliability would simply mean that they rarely break down. How reliable are you and your people and can that reliability be measured within the parameters that you have set?

If we use technology measurements as the benchmarks for understanding how a system, an organization and/or the human element should work, then we can see that certain criteria need to be considered and adjusted. Ultimately, we all want our business and its people to operate successfully. The challenge is to get aligned and make it happen.

Final Thoughts

Used properly, the SET-Ability model will help you and your team establish direction, align your teams, take a structured approach, engage your people, transform your business and get measureable results. It will improve your business, both today and in the future.

PART TWO

Setting the Ground Work

*"There are many questions to ask and people to
meet on the road to your success"*
– Richard Lannon

3

Question Your Business

I think it's natural for any manager to want to grow his business. The question is at what rate, and in what direction, and in what format?
– Wilbur Ross

It's All in the Questions You Ask

Question everything about your business. Good initial questions will help you determine where you are and what you need to focus on. Questions are a critical part of the planning process. The responses you receive will create important dialogue among your planning team, which will help you make better business decisions. For example, consider these three short questions:

Where are you at?
How's it going?
How's it going today?

They are short, simple questions that, believe it or not, should resonate with all business leaders and their team. They cover the state of the business and the business leader's personal state at this point in time. Ultimately, they are what you should ask everyday in the course of your professional and business life. They are at the heart of a business audit or assessment. Think about it—at the end of the day, aren't they what you want to know from your internal teams and the overall business market? These three simple questions are heartbeat questions.

Sources of Business Feedback

Many business leaders feel a sense of unease when they hear words like 'audit,' 'assessment' and 'questionnaire.' These particular words (often used interchangeably) force us to take a candid look at our business and that's not always easy. Yet if done properly, assessments such as these provide an opportunity to engage your people, acquire feedback and gain a deeper understanding of your business.

Concrete feedback about how your business is doing can come from two different sources: external and internal stakeholders. Feedback from external stakeholders—banks, investors, government agencies, professional organizations, family and friends, regulatory bodies, customers, vendors, partnerships, etc.—helps us understand what is at stake in our business. Feedback from internal stakeholders—employees, management teams, and the executive team—is crucial for streamlining working processes and productivity, making tool adjustments, forming our business development efforts and being right with our people.

Taken together, this feedback helps us get real about our business, how it's doing, and what changes need to be made.

A Critical Part of the Process

As uncomfortable as feedback from your stakeholders can be, it's a critical part of the overall process. Your stakeholders are there to help you and the company stay honest and focused, to help you know what you are good at and where you and your business need to improve. Stakeholders set the present state boundaries of your business and keep you honest and humble. Their constructive criticism will also help you understand and identify the areas you need to focus on and improve.

Organizational Structure

Every organization has a structure. This can be a formal or informal, functional, a product organization, a divisional organization, a matrix organization or any combination thereof. But regardless of what type of structure your organization has, it will have these three different levels of operation: strategic, tactical and operational. These levels of the organization are vital to an assessment and are represented here in the following diagram (Figure 3-1):

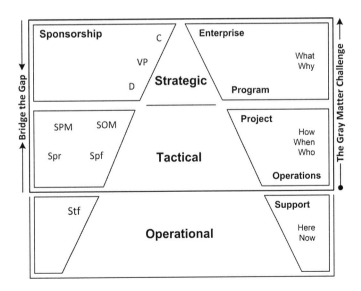

Figure 3-1: Business Organizational and Strategic Structure Perspective (Organizational Levels)

Representations on the diagram:

- C (Chief Officers),
- VP (Vice President)
- D (Directors),
- SPM (Senior Project Managers),
- SOM (Senior Operation Managers),
- Spr (Senior Supervisor)
- Spf (Senior Professional)
- Stf (Staff).

Each stakeholder group has a key responsibility of being strategic, tactical or operational in their scope of work and business perspective. In most businesses, the gap between the strategic and the tactical level often needs to be bridged.

The strategic is the what and why of your business and the tactical is the how, who, when and cost. The gap that exists between the strategic and the tactical is represented by a box drawn around it. The link between the sponsor and the gap is 'The Gray Matter Challenge.' It's the place that you must climb to in order to bridge the gap between the strategic and the tactical. This is represented by the arrow moving upwards from the tactical to the strategic. It's the challenge of raising your thinking and capabilities to the strategic level, as it is so tempting to stay in the tactical (who, what, when) and operational (here and now). Some find it easier to bridge that gap than others, but it must be done.

Levels of Questions

With each level of business structure come questions tailored to that particular level. They are most easily defined as the following:

- **Strategic:** The what and why questions. What are we going to be focusing on? Why is that so important? The why question provides the biggest benefit as it focuses on importance and business value. Together what and why questions engage discussion, establish decisions and create accountability.

- **Tactical:** These are the questions that professionals ask the most. They include who, how, when, and how much. They're perfect for the mid-level planners and people responsible for getting work done – the doing. To be effective in long term planning, however, these questions must be linked to the strategic questions.

- **Operational:** Always fun, as they are the here and now questions. It's like the phone rings and you pick it up, deal with the issue and move onto the next thing. No doubt you use the 'what and why' question as in what do you want and why should I care. But most likely you are the "who"--the one with the know-how—and need to get it done, when.

If you listen carefully to the types of questions people ask in meetings, you can see the distinctions between the strategic and tactical thinkers.

Raising Our Thinking – what and why

As part of the audit process, it is important to establish an overall perspective of your business. This will often involve a new level of thinking for all of the teams in the organization, rising above the operational thinking of the "here and now" and getting the senior members into the discussion of the "what and why." It is often said, "If you can answer why, then you've earned your salary." "Why" is considered the benefit and value question. The

S.E.T. Organizational model represents this lift in thinking and discussion and helps reminds us where we need to focus.

Asking Questions to Understand Your Business

Knowing where you are requires an honest, candid look at your business by the leadership team. That's where a strategic audit or assessment comes into play. There are many kinds of audits or assessment tools in the market place and the challenge is finding the right one for you and your organization, particularly considering where you are at this point and time.

A good place to start in the planning process is to focus on 'what' questions. What questions are extremely powerful tools for thinking about your business strategy, your personal strategy, goals and objectives. The key is to know which questions to ask and to be willing to take a candid look at your business.

7 Questions to Consider

Here are seven candid "what and why " questions that every business leader should ask:

1. **What are the overall strengths and weaknesses of my business? Why?** Strengths and weaknesses exist in all organizations and should include considerations for people, resources, culture, work processes, tools, supply chain, financial situation, etc. Establishing your strengths and weaknesses provides you the opportunity to get clear on where you excel and where you need to improve.

2. **What are the overall opportunities and threats to your business? Why?** Focus here on your external world, the things you cannot control but must be aware of. Some items could include a market shift, retirement,

succession, competitive movement and changes, the global business climate (local, national or international), obstacles and/or climate and weather effects. We often miss the opportunity to do environmental scanning. Look outside your office to truly understand the opportunities and threats to your organization.

3. **What political, economic, social and technological conditions impact your business? Why?** What's happening in your local business scene economically? Is there a product or service that people want or need to buy? Is technology impacting your team and their need for training? What important social change will impact the business? Are you developing leaders for tomorrow? Every answer should lead to another question. Dig deeply, exhaust yourself and find people to help you through this process.

4. **What do you want to achieve, protect, avoid and eliminate? Why?** This question contains all the elements of risk planning. There are always things we want to achieve, protect, avoid and eliminate on a personal, team or organizational basis. What are they? Identify as many as possible and make a list. Examples vary, but could include such things as increased sales, keeping an established portfolio, avoiding trouble or accidents, establishing an employee health program or helping people drop a few pounds. The point here is that whatever is identified must be relevant to your business and its challenges.

5. **What are the key challenges you face today, tomorrow and in the distant future? Why?** We're in an era where we must be predictive and adaptive. Strategic planning is about timeframes with past, present and future

considerations. Establish what your work world should look like within these different timeframes. Planning used to focus on 5 to 15 year cycles. That has changed. Many organizations focus on 3 to 5 year plans. Some find is difficult to look beyond 3 years. Now we must keep our eye on short-term road trips along with long term implications.

6. **What are our honest business coordinates? Our actual location? Why?** This isn't a question about physical location per se. It's more about your relative location in relation to your competitors and the market. Its intent is to force pure honesty. It's used to establish your present situation and to help you accept complete responsibility and accountability for it. No blame-storming allowed. Outside forces might have contributed, but at some point decisions were made to set your direction. As a business leader, you were either active or reactive and there were consequences either way. Capture it, leverage it and be prepared to let it go.

7. **What key initiatives are going to be placed on the strategic agenda of your business? Why?** A strategy agenda item is a high level plan of action item designed to achieve a vision. It is defined as a 'Plan of Action.' At some point you will need to make key decisions that will make a difference in your business. The upper level decisions will become your strategic agenda items.

Honesty is a Challenge

To really know where you want to go in the long term, it will be important to find the questions that will help you become more honest about your business. Consider using the above question list when you start the planning process. The initial responses will assist you in setting the stage for good discussion and create the foundation for your business benchmark.

The essence of being honest or candid about your business is that it keeps you real, particularly when you take both an internal and external look. Part of the assessment process is to get that input from internal and external stakeholders, so that you have a clearer picture as to where you are at. You will know what you are about from all different perspectives. This, in turn, allows the business leadership to get focused on the things it needs to talk about.

A Snapshot Speaks a 1000 Words

The whole point of questioning your business is to get an entire snapshot of the business as it stands right now. This snapshot will enable you and your team to understand all the moving parts, how they work together, and what impact they're having on one another and on the business as a whole. By engaging in a combination of questionnaires and one-on-one interviews with the key people in your workplace, you'll be able to put together much of the information you need to create a working snapshot that is the initial benchmark for where you are presently. Benchmarking also allows you to compare your business to the world around you. This comparison can be both internal and external.

One of the things that should be noted is that this assessment process does not need to be an exhausting exercise. It seems way too easy for business leaders and professional companies to become busy doing endless assessments and report writing that no one reads or cares about. To assess accurately, you need to work in draft mode and move forward with working copies: your business is a living machine with moving, breathing parts. Treat it that way and stay flexible. Today we have to work on a constant go and benchmark on the move. Don't be afraid of that. When the line in the sand moves, you merely need to re-establish that line. It's best to be candid and get it done on the move, rather than stop everything and create a static result.

Once you get everyone's feedback, you can then move forward with strategic planning meetings, engaging your people through using the SET-Ability model and getting the business leadership team talking.

Knowing What You Need

Are you interested in redefining the organization or business identity? Better understanding the environment in which you operate internally and externally? Improving the products and services that you offer? Maybe you're interested in what you produce and provide to the market place, the level of innovation, reinvention and renewal that exists within your business. Perhaps your focus needs to be among your people, your performance measures, your productivity and process effectiveness and your business leadership team.

These all come together to form your overall business impact. Good or bad, it just is. You need to develop the list of items to discuss, review them and then make your key business decisions based on them. The end result we're looking for is to make better business decisions and move forward into clear, focused plans.

Knowing When to Stop

You will also need to consider which feedback you want to consider for your strategic focus. As we've established, there are many things to consider when looking at understanding your business environments--many moving parts. Be careful of not becoming stuck through asking too many questions, having too much information and not being able to make a decision (also known as the paralysis of analysis). The best thing to do is discipline yourself, set time boundaries and pull back in your questioning when needed so you can move forward.

Final Thoughts

If you try to move from strategic plans to tactical and practical operations without a clear, focused plan in place, you will flounder. Use an audit, assessments or questionnaires to help you determine your present state and areas of focus.

They put a stick in your hand. And without a stick in your hand you cannot place it or draw a line in the sand. Without a line drawn or a boundary set, you will not know what to focus on or why. You will not be able to have those difficult conversations. You will be stranded, waiting for the next wave to hit and wash the line away. And then you'll need to start again.

4

Stakeholders have Business Impact

So much business is based on the belief that we should do whatever we can within legal limits to make as much money as we can. Ben & Jerry's was based on values, and we try to operate a business that not just sells ice cream but partners with all our stakeholders - whether that's suppliers or customers - to bring about a more sustainable world.

– Jerry Greenfield

People Opinions and Impact are Everywhere

A lot of people—both individuals and groups—impact your business. In fact, it's safe to say that just about everyone impacts your business. We call these people stakeholders. A stakeholder is any person or organization who can be positively or negatively impacted by, or cause an impact on the actions of a company, government, or organization. Your job is to be clear on who they are and what impact and influence they truly have.

Stakeholders – Internal and External to the Organization

Knowing your stakeholders and their impact and influence on your business will help you get the most out of your strategic planning. This, in turn, will allow you to achieve stronger positive outcomes. Then it's just a matter of what level of involvement you want them to have in the planning process, the various levels you want to engage them at, and the people you want on your planning team.

When evaluating who should be a part of your planning team, it is important to consider all the key elements and people that need to be involved. This can be done through a combination of profiling, strategic assessments and stakeholders' analysis. Stakeholder analysis is a systematic process that is used to gather and analyze information to identify and understand the interests, motivations, impact and influence of a particular group of people. One of the primary reasons you engage in stakeholder analysis is to understand each player's level of influence, importance and impact.

Whether you are starting from scratch or updating an existing plan, you will need to go through the process of understanding your stakeholders' influence, importance and impact early on in the planning and business analysis process. This will not only allow for better current business decisions all the way around, but it will also help you navigate the road ahead.

Internal and External Stakeholders

In the SET-Ability model, we can see that external and internal stakeholders are represented on the first and second bar:

Stakeholders – Internal and External to the Organization		
Organization	Teams	Individuals

Internal Stakeholders

Internal stakeholders are people in your business who are committed to serving your organization. They could include employees, temporary contractors and staff, volunteers, board members, hired professionals, and/or family members. Often, they are categorized as individuals, grouped in teams, and/or organized as departments as part of the initial planning preparation.

By definition, each internal stakeholder has an interest in the business. Employees might want to earn more money, have better benefits, have job stability, be respected and treated well, or have better communication. The leadership and investors might be interested in increased profit, investment, earning income, or the changes that need to be made to get to the next level in business. Regardless of their agenda, however, all internal stakeholders have influence and impact on the business.

There are often a number of options when considering which stakeholders to engage internally. You can engage by position, role and responsibility, and/or by group, and/or by department level. Position often generally refers to the title and job descriptions people carry. Role and responsibility has more to do with what people really do – the many hats that they wear as they work. You may have been assigned or volunteered for other roles and responsibilities than your title describes. For example, being part of the department hiring committee review team. (Role and responsibilities and position are not always the same thing.)

Depending on how your organization is structured, you could also choose to go by group or department. Traditional organizations might go by department and engage the senior team leadership/management team. By group could mean you are a regionalized organization that is willing to include managers and senior people from other parts of the organization.

Some companies have fewer options and have to do the best with what they have, meaning they do not always have the right people in strategic positions or they employ people who do not have strategic thinking abilities. If possible, however, you should do your best to make sure that the business development, finance, human resources, operations, manufacturing, production and technology departments are all represented. In the end, the size of your company will dictate your internal stakeholder considerations.

External Stakeholders

External stakeholders are organizations, groups and individuals outside of your business that are impacted by the consequences and outcomes of your decisions. They include government bodies, investors, a board of directors, unions, customers and/or special interest groups. They can have a significant impact and/or influence on your business, and can sometimes even constrain your business. It is important, therefore, not to underestimate them. For example, your customers probably have one of the biggest influences on your business.

There are lots of examples where a company built a product, brought it to market and it never sold. Or they discovered that they're ahead of the curve and the customer was not yet ready to receive the product. A little investigative work could have prevented the company from creating a product that the customer was not ready to buy, but this step had been overlooked and the company paid dearly for it. Even today, many companies don't include the voice of the customer (VoC) when it comes to planning, even though their customers have a huge impact on the company.

Other external stakeholders can even include family and friends. Imagine the president has an outside friend or confidant as an advisor—that person has impact. That confidant could directly or indirectly influence the direction of the organization. For example, what if the confident had a background in finance and the company was seeking to re-finance or invest in another part of the organization? Chances are the president of the company would seek out their advice prior to making any decision. As a confident they may very well have personal interest and motivation that should be considered in the overall whole.

Stakeholder Analysis Tools

Stakeholder analysis tools help you to determine who should be on your planning team, as well as the importance of stakeholders in general. Generally there are three types of stakeholders. These include:

- **Primary stakeholders:** those ultimately affected, either positively or negatively by an organization's actions.
- **Secondary stakeholders:** the 'intermediaries.' Persons or organizations indirectly affected by an organization's actions.
- **Key stakeholders:** have significant influence upon or importance within an organization (and can also belong to the first two groups).[9]

With that understanding you can learn to apply some common stakeholder analysis tools.

The Stakeholder Matrix Fulfilled

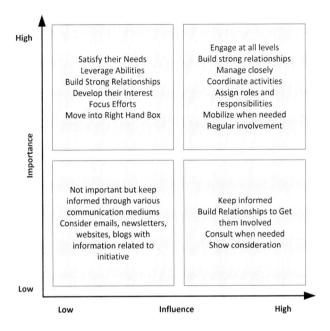

Figure 4-1: The Stakeholder Matrix with possible approaches

One of the tools we can use to understand the role stakeholders play in our organization is called a stakeholder matrix. A stakeholder matrix is used to map the power, influence and importance a group of stakeholders has on your organization and/or your key initiatives and projects. If used properly, it can be a very powerful tool.

The following is a four quadrants stakeholder matrix that is used for understanding the relationship of stakeholder importance, power and influence.

- High Importance and High Power and Influence: make sure you engage closely and influence actively

- High Importance and Low Power and Influence: make sure you keep them satisfied
- Low Importance and High Power and Influence: may sure you keep them informed
- Low Importance and Low Power and Influence: make sure you monitor and invest minimum effort satisfying this stakeholder group[10]

Consider a team—perhaps a hockey team. The larger the team (i.e. the more moving parts) the greater the stakeholder understanding required. Like your business, players on a hockey team need to work together efficiently. Chaos between the players and how they work together spells defeat on the ice. On top of that, there is a host of other stakeholders involved: managers, coaches, fans, owners, etc.

The more all of these parties can be aligned towards a common goal (winning a game or perhaps ranking top in their league), the better chance the team has of achieving that goal. To do this effectively, we need to understand where each stakeholder belongs and how they fit into the overall planning process.

The Stakeholder Triangle Connection

Stakeholder triangles are used to understand the one-to-one relationships that exist among stakeholder groups. A simple triangle might include the client, the vendor and the contractor. The contractor agrees with the vendor to provide services to the client. There are three one-to-one connections that need to be managed. These relationships can be either simple or complex, depending on the arrangement and communication requirements.

With multiple stakeholders you get multiple one-to-one relationships. For a sports team, these might be the fans, management team, investors, city or government support, private vendors, etc. All have a part in the business's success. Even the hotdog vendor has an impact on the team and the business.

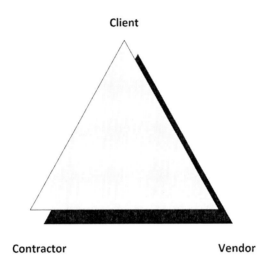

Figure 4-2: The Stakeholder Triangle

The Triangle Web We Weave

Complex relationships within your organization can also be modeled using triangles. Imagine that you added a lawyer, human resources, information technology, corporate services, finance, field workers, unions, special interest groups, etc. to the picture. Now it truly becomes complex, yet if you use stakeholder triangles, you end up with a number of interlocking triangles knitted together like a web, allowing you to see the one-to-one relationships among them.

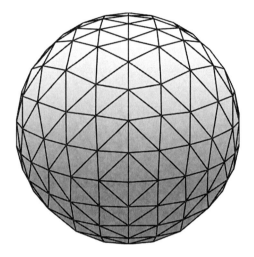

**Figure 4-3: The Stakeholder Sphere representing
complex relationships.**

In many ways it's like a complex spider web that can be simplified into smaller parts. And like a spider web, every link can be either strong or weak. Any broken link or large gap can create weakness in the entire system.

When the lines that create joined triangles have no breaks in them, the overall relationship is strong. But have you ever noticed that if you break a link or a main stem of a spider web it disintegrates and starts to fall apart? Something gets lost in the broken connections. It's the same within a business with interconnecting triangles that form a web. If you break an interconnecting link, a gap forms making the overall structure and relationships between stakeholders weaker. It is through this level of stakeholder analysis you can understand interest, motivation, stakeholder objectives and business impact in complex systems.

Common Considerations

Stakeholder analysis, profiling, and strategic assessments are all tools intended help you to understand your stakeholders.

Stakeholder Analysis

As mentioned before, stakeholder analysis is performed both at the start of new projects and/or when there is a need to clarify the consequences of proposed changes in the organization. It's crucial to a business's success, not only because it brings to light exactly who your stakeholders are and what kind of impact they can have, but also because it focuses on developing cooperation between the stakeholders and the project team, ultimately assuring successful outcomes for key business initiatives and projects.

Stakeholder Profiles

Another way to better understand the role of individual stakeholders is through profiling. Profiling gives you an insider's perspective into the way people act and what they see as their objectives, allowing you to better see how they'll fit into the planning process and what impact they may have overall. What they do and why they do it is important for your whole team to understand, especially prior to planning and working together to create new direction. You can use profiling to create insight into stakeholder's natural inclinations and the way they impact their peers, the decision-making processes, and the actions they will take.

Planning Abilities

When it comes to planning team selection, you need to consider personality versus position. Keep in mind, however, that sometimes position has little to do with a person's strategic planning abilities. A good fit has a lot more to do with the type of person they are and the role(s) and responsibilities they take on than mere position.

Some people are naturally strategic and others are more tactical or task-based. Sometimes you do not have the option in terms of who is on your planning team (i.e. you must include senior people). That 's expected. The challenge is to focus on raising their thinking, taking them from the tactical (how, who, when) to the strategic (what and why) as outlined previously. This can be done through the focused application of effective strategic facilitation techniques.

A Relationship with the Business

Sometimes you may have a family-versus-business dynamic at play and that can complicate matters. If the family is a high-functioning unit, then you are fortunate and enjoy the ride to greater success. If there is a lot of infighting, on the other hand, the road will be bumpy at best. Some upfront thinking and planning can help the business through these challenges.

Family-integrated businesses can sometimes be the most challenging to lead through the strategic planning and roadmap process, as the line between the business and the family obligations has a stronger connection. There are many personal interests, motivations and contradicting goals that need to be worked out. Often it requires a number of one-on-one discussions to flesh out the issues and to address them appropriately. (This is when the use of an outside facilitator is especially beneficial.)

Upfront Feedback

A strategic assessment with open-ended questions will help get you and your internal stakeholders thinking about the business, what is going on, and dialoguing on the business issues. You will find that presenting the right questions upfront and putting them into a summary of findings will assist you in the process.

Create a Common Stakeholders List

Creating a stakeholder list will help you ensure that you do not miss any. Here are a few to consider:

- ☐ Clients
- ☐ Customers
- ☐ Subject Matter Experts
- ☐ Future Planners
- ☐ System Specialists
- ☐ Administration
- ☐ Technical Professionals
- ☐ Potential Users
- ☐ Sales People
- ☐ Marketing People
- ☐ Style Designers
- ☐ Graphics Artists
- ☐ Usability Experts
- ☐ Safety Professionals
- ☐ Maintenance Technician
- ☐ Look Designers
- ☐ Manufacturer
- ☐ Product Installer
- ☐ Training Staff
- ☐ Project Management
- ☐ Business Analysts
- ☐ Requirements Specialists
- ☐ Technical Designers
- ☐ Systems Architect
- ☐ Organisational Designers
- ☐ Negative Stakeholders
- ☐ Regulator
- ☐ Special Committees

- ☐ Security Officers
- ☐ Human Resources
- ☐ Lawyers
- ☐ Environmentalist
- ☐ Executive Team Members

- ☐ Public Opinion
- ☐ Testing Professionals
- ☐ Auditor Department
- ☐ Investors
- ☐ Purchasing Specialist

Sometimes the hardest decision to make is not to include a particular stakeholder in the process, or to make sure to include a key stakeholder who tends to have challenging insight or a negative critique is invited. There is no hard, fast rule as to whom you should or should not include. Just remember that leaving individuals or a stakeholder group out because they challenge you or do not share your views may be inappropriate. Part of planning is hearing the difficult feedback. Just be prepared to understand your stakeholders, know their impact, figure out where they fit and how best to engage and manage them.

Through some up front planning and stakeholder analysis, you can avoid having the wrong people engaged.

Stakeholder Dilemma

There are many things to consider when deciding who should be involved in the planning process. The real challenge is ensuring—to the best of your ability—that you have the best people engaged. You want the people that truly represent the business and have its highest good at the forefront of their thinking. In particular, it's important to understand the key stakeholders' one-to-one relationships *vis-a-vis* the business dynamics.

Stakeholder analysis for planning and analysis purposes does not need to be complicated. It can be done in a meeting room on a white board. Discussions should be around identifying groups and representation, both internally and externally. Questions should be asked about each individual's participation and the impact they will have. The key is to look for the gaps in the stakeholder requirements, the one-to-one relationships, and their impact.

Align Your Organization

As you go through the pre-planning process it will become apparent that you need to align your organization with your key stakeholders. Aligning your organization in this sense means making sure that the different levels—the strategic, tactical and operational—are all working together towards the same purpose. This holds particularly true for internal stakeholder organization.

Most alignment happens at the organizational, team and individual levels of the business. At this point you're really looking at who should have a seat at the table. And while it's important to identify who should be involved, it's just as important to address what they bring to the planning session and why that is so important to you.

Planned Communications

It's also important to pre-plan your communications so that they include both internal and external stakeholder groups, regardless of whether they'll be involved or not. Remember, not everyone should be involved. Often organizations make the mistake of inviting the wrong stakeholders to planning sessions, thereby causing unnecessary conflict or off-topic discussions. One of the most common mistakes is to place tactical thinkers at strategic meetings. Tactical thinkers tend to talk tasks and will often make a statement asking someone else to tell them what to do. They will talk about the how, who, when of the business, not the bigger picture needed for strategic planning.

Types of Thinkers

Strategic thinkers will challenge one another and focus on the what and why of the business. That is what's needed here. If you have too many tactical thinkers at a strategic planning meeting, you can end up with a tactical plan, not a strategic one. If you're a tactical-based business who spends more time in the how, who and when, this might be ok in the short term, but if your business is needing to be more strategic, this could derail your strategic planning. Yet moving from being a tactical business to a strategic business can be a real challenge. Being strategic sometimes means developing your tactical thinkers into strategic thinkers and this isn't a natural progression for everyone.

Final Thoughts

Remember, you won't always have all the right people, especially when we are in smaller businesses. You just do the best with what we have.

PART THREE

Know Where You Want to Go

"Accept Yourself in the Present.
See Yourself in the Future. Do it with Purpose."
– Richard Lannon

5

Vision and Mission for the Future

A mission statement is not something you write overnight... But fundamentally, your mission statement becomes your constitution, the solid expression of your vision and values. It becomes the criterion by which you measure everything else in your life.
– Stephen Covey

The Foundation to Every Business: Know Where You are Going

At some point every organization should consider what they are about and where they are going. In the business world this is called having a vision and mission. Vision and mission are at the foundation of good planning. Not only do they tie directly into your strategic next steps, they anchor your decision making by providing a sense of purpose and direction.

Vision – Mission	Values – Principles – Goals - Objectives

Imagine for a moment that your stakeholders, either internal or external, couldn't articulate what your organization or business is all about. This would have a negative impact on your business, as no one would be able to communicate your overall purpose, either to themselves or to others. Without a clear vision and mission, people will not know what to focus on. Vision and mission provide clarity of purpose and can transform the way people see your organization. They should be something that stirs the emotions, is universally understood, and makes them people willing to share them with others.

> *If you don't know where it is you want to go,*
> *how are you going to get there?*

A well thought-out vision and mission will help guide your business. They will provide the glue that hold things together. They should also help keep you honest and aligned with the key business and stakeholder requirements that make your business successful. If they don't, it may be time for an update—a vision and mission audit to ensure you are what you say you are and that you're still on track.

Foresight (vision) and clarity of purpose (mission) are at the forefront of good planning, regardless of whether you're working on strategic, tactical or operational levels. And since your business can be impacted at a click of a button in today's world of instant and very public communication, you and your people need to be especially clear on what your business is about.

Something Important to Consider

Many, many business professionals have told me that vision and mission are all fluff. In their experience, people and organizations create a mission and vision and then don't adhere to them. (This is something important for organizations to consider and remember. Your stakeholders expect you to walk your talk.)

To those people who think vision and mission is all fluff, I might ask, do you really want to be a part of a company that does not adhere to their purpose, that lacks a sense of direction, and that doesn't know where they are going or what they are all about? Consider it. Why work for or be part of an organization that lacks clarity or something that you can connect with?

Vision and mission are meant to connect people. Throughout history, every movement, every event, every great idea made connections with people through a sense of vision and mission. **They stood on purpose.**

Know Where You're Going

Everyone needs a mission and a vision for their success. They provide something we can connect with, something we can believe in. They allow us to reach our wholeness. They help us to get to where we want to go and provide focus for the people on board with us. There are many great examples of vision and mission statements within community, public and private business organizations. Here are two companies have clearly articulated a combination of both vision and mission:

> "PepsiCo's responsibility is to continually improve all aspects of the world in which we operate - environment, social, economic - creating a better tomorrow than today. Our vision is put into action through programs and a focus on environmental stewardship, activities to benefit society, and a commitment to build shareholder value by making PepsiCo a truly sustainable company."[11]

> "Our [Amazon's] vision is to be earth's most customer centric company; to build a place where people can come

to find and discover anything they might want to buy online."[12]

Pepsi Cola's vision is seeking to create a better tomorrow than today. This statement alone forces their people to consider the actions they are taking. Since they added the environment (social and economic) into their statement, it opens the doors for their external stakeholders—their customers and public— to ensure they live up to that promise. (It would be interesting to see in what way this company is invested into environmental stewardship and other activities to benefit society per their vision, and what their stakeholders have to say about their level of success.) If they're living up to their vision and mission statement, then Pepsi Cola is a company that should be on the positive radar screen of all generations, past and future.

Amazon has made it easy to shop from home. They've provided an experience that allows a customer to locate the product they would like, order it and have it delivered to their doorstep. It's reminiscent of the days of when you would thumb through the Sears' or Eaton's catalogues and order what you need for your family via the mail. Today's difference is that you can order online and the product will comes to your home in a matter of days. Amazon continues to break new ground with their on-line business model of being customer-focused and ensuring people can get everything they want from one place – Amazon.com.

Community Based Organizations

Imagine, for a moment, that you represent a community-based organization like a church, community center, non-profit club or health organization. Chances are, you're part of that organization because you believe in their purpose. But what if their purpose was not well defined, out-dated, or not defined at all? How would you know what to believe in?

Years ago, when working with a church, we discovered that the vision and mission needed to be revisited. The organization had matured and was about to go through a leadership transition. This church served a specific geographic community and competed for participants with other churches in their community.

To address the issue, we ran a vision and mission session with the key leadership, revisiting the foundational core of the church and what it wanted to accomplish in the future. They discovered that the church needed to remain grounded in community principles and build on community programming. They also found that their combined vision and mission was about "living life together."

In turn, once the vision and mission were solidified, the people were provided with something to rally around and could then develop appropriate community-based programming to serve their specific area and community needs. They now had focus and were able to offer solutions to local community challenges through "living life together." We often don't think of a church as a business, but visioning and missioning works for anyone who wants to be effective in their endeavours.

What's the Difference

Vision is often confused with mission, but they are actuality quite different from one another. Vision statements are future-based and are meant to inspire and give direction to the employees of the company. They are an internal resource that helps the company know where it's going. A mission statement, on the other hand, is a present-based statement designed to convey a sense of why the company exists—both to members of the company and to the community at large. The mission statement is foundational. It is core-based. It is purpose. A mission statement answers the question, "Why does my business exist?" A vision statement answers, "Where do I see my business going?" Often times they get mixed together and are therefore a challenge to distinguish from one another.

It is difficult to have vision without a mission and vise versa. It's great to have vision, but what if it isn't anchored in anything worthwhile? It's also great to have a mission and know what you are all about, but what if you can't execute it? Really, who cares what it is you want to achieve unless you can say why you want to achieve it?

Vision and mission relate to one another directly. Your job as a business leader and senior management team is to define them, own them, provide them, use them, live them and make them happen.

Mission vs. Vision

Since 1990 I've had a mission to **invest in the success of other people and organizations**. My mission can be summed up in three key words: Structure, Engage and Transform. That is to say, structure your approach, engage your people and transform your business. Throughout the years, this mission has helped me and my company stay on course.

My vision of success, on the other hand, has changed over time as key career, business and personal milestones were achieved. Years ago my vision of success had to do with my career, family and health. In my formative career years I saw myself in senior management running a large geographic territory for one of the big four firms. I'd achieve that by my mid-thirties. These days my vision of success is to be a focused, virtual enterprise providing strategic facilitation, business speaking, training and coaching services that provide value for my clients and maximum flexibility, while supporting my mission. As you can see, over time my mission has not changed, but my vision has.

Knowing Your Vision

There are many stories on the importance of vision, some of the biggest of which come from companies like Starbucks, MicroSoft and Apple. "A coffee in everyone's hand" and "A computer in every household" are great examples—they are clear vision-style statements that describe what the companies want to achieve. In these cases it was something big, something that did not yet exist, something that would change the world.

Even Coca Cola had a vision at one time—you can see it in their older commercials where they say they would like to "buy the world a Coke and keep it company." Nestled within statement was the vision of consumption of Coca Cola on a global scale, where people shared. We all know their success. They knew what they wanted to achieve, and they made it happen by using their vision statement as a declaration of their company's mid-term and long-term goals.

A Vision Statement

A vision statement can range from one line to several paragraphs and identifies what the company would like to achieve or accomplish. A good vision statement provides the inspiration for the daily operation of a business, its strategic decisions and its project's integration. Whether your vision statement is several paragraphs or just one line, it's always best to craft it in a way where people--your people--can remember it easily. That is why I like **vision statements that have the same amount of words as your phone number: ten. Seven keywords and three more that make the statement pop out.**

Keep Things Dynamic

Vision statements are dynamic and can change over time. As a company grows, its objectives and goals may change. As a result, **vision statements will need to be occasionally revised** as goals are met. At the same time, they should be written to last for at least a few years. **Your mission statement**, on the other hand, **should** be written to **last a lifetime**. Your business or organization's mission should be foundational and be core to its existence.

You and Your People Need It

Know Your Mission

A mission is enduring; it should be at least 20 to 100 years strong. Everyone needs a mission. Imagine if you truly understood what your purpose in life is. Most entrepreneurs and business leaders do. They have a sense of their anchor, whether intrinsically understood or extrinsically stated. Stakeholders also need to know what you are about--they want to know your mission. You may have an internal sense of your mission, but if you're not communicating it, this can create challenges in you business.

Having worked with thousands of entrepreneurs, business leaders, senior management teams and professionals, the ones that are most successful know what it is they are about and how they fit into the bigger picture.

Know Your Vision

Just as with knowing your mission, it's also important to have a strong, defined sense of your vision. Your vision of success is what drives your business or organization, whether it is for profit, not-for-profit or public-based. There is usually something that you want to accomplish. Better yet, *need* to accomplish. Vision allows you to take a journey to where you need to go. At the same time, it must always be anchored in your mission.

Steps You Can Take

How to create a mission statement that has both life and vitality? One way is hold a brainstorming session centered on the following questions:

1. Who are we? (Focusing on internal relationships)
2. Whom do we serve? (I.e. who are our stakeholders?)
3. What do we do? (I.e. what business are we in?)
4. How do we do it? (What are the values by which we operate?)

Next, turn the answers to these questions into a mission statement that anchors your organization or project. Your people can and should be able to do this, and having them do so will both help them have a sense of being connected, as well as breathe life into what you and your organization is all about.

Creating a Vision Statement

Imagine that you're reading a newspaper five years from now and that the front pages of *Global Mail*, *The National Post*, *The New York Times*, *or The Wall Street Journal* have big news about your company. Imagine that this is the best possible news you could ever read. Write down the headline of the story and the main points of the story. Make sure you include the critical decisions the company has made in the past ten years to reach this point. (Don't worry, you can always change the time frame.)

Consider these questions:

- What does the article highlight about your organization?
- What does it say about the uniqueness about your organization?
- What services does it report that you are providing?
- What does it tell you about how you're changed in the past five years?
- What is the recognizable condition you would hope to have in place in the next five years?

Change any timeframes or items that help you build on these ideas.

Fitting in with Your Stakeholders

Establish a Culture

Many companies have used their vision and mission to establish the culture they want in their organization, both internally and externally. For example, a community-based organization decided to focus on creating relationships in the local community. They established a culture based on one statement—living healthy lives together. The organization developed programs that addressed the community's needs and interests around this topic. People within the organization were coached and mentored on the creation of a culture that focused on the community's success. In turn, staff and volunteers became innovative in their approach to supporting one another and the community.

The culture transformed into a caring, community-driven environment. This became apparent in the feedback from staff, volunteers and the community at large. People felt included, important and connected.

What you say you are about, where you want to go and the way you walk that talk connects people and builds community and your business culture.

Guide a Decision

Your vision and mission statements can be used to guide business decisions. For example, a mid-range technology company used their vision and mission as a guide for when they chose a vendor for their human resource and management consulting needs. They interviewed three potential vendors and looked at what those vendors were all about. As part of the exercise, they also had discussions with the senior management of each firm to determine how closely the vendors had enabled and aligned with their own vision and mission. The one that was hired was selected for not just how closely they fit, but also how well they could support and impact the vision and mission of the client company.

People and Performance

People and performance are negatively impacted when companies do not have a vision or mission statement. For example, a natural resource service firm realized they didn't have a vision and mission in place that supported the organization's human capital needs. This issue was negatively impacting their hiring practices and ability to pay bonuses against their key performance criteria. At the time, the hiring and bonus payments were random, like throwing darts at a wall, as they really didn't have any standards to link them to. They then embarked on the journey to create a clear vision and mission statement as part of their overall strategic planning process. Once they put the proper statements together, they were able to share what they were all about with stakeholders much more easily. Once the vision and mission statements were created, they were also able to standardize programs for hiring, compensating, and training their people.

Rowing in the Same Direction

The senior management team needs to truly buy into what the organization is all about. That buy-in happens through a well thought-out vision and mission statement. If members of your senior management and/or support teams do not connect with what your organization is about, then they probably shouldn't be part of your organization. They'll only work against what your organization is seeking to accomplish. For vision and mission truly to work, everyone needs to be fully onboard. If they aren't, then stop the boat and let them get off.

If your organization, business leadership team, mid-level management and/or employees are not aligned to your business's purpose, it may well be that the connections between the vision and mission have not yet been made and/or your stakeholders are not convinced--they think it is fluff. The challenge is that you need those words to make strategic, clear-standing linkages to key business impact zones and the results you want to achieve. Your stakeholders need to be a part of it and know that you as the business leader and your team live by it. And most importantly, you yourself need to be behind it.

Final Thoughts

It's very difficult to plan the success of other parts of your business without clarity of mission (what you are all about) and vision (what it is you want to achieve). There are many impacts—both positive and negative—related to vision and mission. The reality is that today, this very day, you would not be where you are without foresight and a sense of purpose. As business leaders and senior management, it is imperative that you ensure you have clarity of purpose and foresight, that you live it, and that you communicate it to your stakeholders. Everyone needs to be on the bus and going in the same direction.

6

Values and Guiding Principles

Values are principles and ideas that bring meaning to the seemingly mundane experience of life. A meaningful life that ultimately brings happiness and pride requires you to respond to temptations as well as challenges with honour, dignity, and courage.
– Laura Schlessinger

The Foundation of Business Decision Making

Core values and guiding principles are two elements that are foundational to your entire organization.

Vision – Mission	Values – Principles	Goals - Objectives

Values are what you believe and base your business on. Examples include adjectives such as dependable, reliable, loyal, innovative, honest, passionate and so on.

Guiding principles are statements which provide the framework for making better business decisions. For example, attracting, developing, and retaining a competent, creative, and highly motivated workforce.

Together they form a set of statements and accepted guidelines that capture how your people should act, work, make decisions, set priorities and conduct themselves. It is imperative to actively set and communicate your core values and principles. If you don't, they will set themselves over time through employee habits. It is my belief that in order to get along in this business world and make successful key decisions, we need to know our values and guiding principles inside and out, and hold to them. It's the only true constant. (Or at least it should be.)

Values and guiding principles also provide the foundation for planning. They're the basis of all decisions and actions. Imagine your company having no values or guiding principles—it would be like being without a soul or heart and/or being dead inside. People would be making choices that create incongruences in your business, since nothing would really matter. All levels of your organization would be impacted. Do you have a set of values and guiding principles that support and enable who you really are in your business?

Like you're business, values and guiding principles are alive. They may grow and change over time as the business matures. It doesn't mean we've left them behind. Rather, we may need to revisit them to see whether they're still applicable today. As your business matures, especially when it is going through a strategic planning process or a project initiative, it's important to determine if the guidelines that served you before still apply now.

Representing Your Organization

Consider team sports--hockey, football, soccer, baseball, etc. The game, the teams and the rules of the game change over time. Even the values of the key stakeholders change. What was acceptable

10, 15 or 20 years ago regarding how a team operates and the way decisions are made on or off the field (or ice) may not be acceptable today.

Yet every team has a set of values and guiding principles around what that team is about, what the sport is about, in what way team members are to represent themselves as part of the team and in what way decisions are to be made. When there is an impasse, there are advisory committees to settle things off the field and referees to make the call on the field. And there is impact if the rules aren't followed. Pretty much all of the decisions are based on a pre-determined approach to the play, to the game and to the industry. These are the values and guiding principles by which the team must operate and make key decisions.

No Guidelines to Follow

Some companies don't have stated values and guiding principles. They may still have them internally, but they remain trapped in the intent of the leadership team. Trapped values and guiding principles are those that exist in the mind of the business leader(s), but haven't been communicated to the rest of the organization.

The challenge with trapped values and guiding principles is that they can create a negative impact on the business. If they are trapped, it's difficult to create a linkage with your performance requirements and what the company is about. This lack of linkage will make it a challenge to manage people against a set of key performance indicators and the expected and appropriate behaviour within the organization. People will not know or understand what is expected of them. In effect, there are no guidelines to follow.

A Health Service Company

A health service company had generally stayed the same since its inception; it was now going on its 25th year of operation. As the leadership team started the process of strategic planning, their mission, vision, values and guiding principles were revisited.

In the initial briefing we began with the question, "Are the present values and guiding principles we have today relevant for where we want to go tomorrow?" As the planning process unfolded, it became clear that adjustments needed to be made— the values and guiding principles needed to reflect something that was more fitting for the future state of the business. That doesn't mean they lost something. It just means that the business had matured and in that maturity it was time to let elements of the past go. They needed to embrace the success they had become and move toward the future they desired. In order to do so, they needed to restate their values and guiding principles and apply them as a litmus test against the business decisions they were going to make and the culture they wanted to create.

They landed on five values and five guiding principles. The one that spoke to everyone the most was *good for the client, good for the system, good for the company.* Now, whenever there is a decision on the table, the senior management team asks whether what they are proposing is *good for the client, good for the system,* and *good for the company* and applies it as a litmus test. That is a powerful understanding of how to use guiding principles.

What it all meant for this Health Care Organization:

Values:

- *Caring, Relationship, Quality, Accountability, and Teamwork*

Guiding Principles:

- *"Good for the client" keeps the company and its people focused on their primary responsibility: the health and well being of their clients.*
- *"Good for the system" is about embracing and enhancing the healthcare system over the long term. Provide benefit and value to the healthcare industry.*
- *"Good for company" has to do with the business side of the organization and sustainability. That means helping patients and maintaining a healthy company over the long term.*[13]

This healthcare organization definitively embraced the portion of planning that is focused on defining your core values and guiding principles. And now, as a company of 25 years, they have grown and developed a set of guiding principles for their business decision-making process that can be used over the long term. A great lesson learned from a company that is a business champion and success.

A Resource Company

Values and guiding principles are an important part of developing key performance requirements, as well as being a key part of your performance management system. A mining company had grown out of the will of the business owner, the CEO. The senior management team was comprised of a very successful group of dedicated professionals, but their employees did not understand what they were all about.

Decisions were being made on the mid- and lower levels that negatively impacted the business, and when it came time to pay bonuses or do performance management, it was like throwing a dart at the wall—there was again no way to measure performance. This also came across in the strategic planning process. The Human Resource department was clambering for something to anchor the performance management system. It quickly became apparent that it was time for the senior management team to articulate what they were all about. In the end, this company came together as a team and created something they could believe in. They established values and guiding principles they could use in moving forward.

What it all meant for this Mining Resource Company:

Values:

- *Service Excellence, People Engagement, Integrity, Commitment and Innovation*

Guiding Principles:

- *Make quality and pride in every solution; Treat people with dignity and respect; All our relationships are based on honesty, respect and fairness; Being loyal to our organization and to our customer; Quality and innovation keep us ahead.*[14]

Once they solidified their guiding principles, they used them to work with their employees, customers and vendors. They used their values and guiding principles as a reference point to judge whether what they were looking at really made sense and aligned with what the company was about. They also used them as guidelines for what they expected from their people, creating a performance management system anchored in their values and guiding principles. In turn, this provided them the ability to getting everyone on the same page, ensuring that all decision-making was based on what the company believed.

Linked Together

As we went through the revisiting and/or creation process in both of these cases, the Executive Team questioned the importance of getting clarity on their definitions of values and guiding principles. Fortunately, there were a few senior managers who understood and supported the process and five core values emerged in each organization, along with five core guiding principles.

They connected the dots and saw the linkage between who they say they are, what they are all about and the principles they use to make business decisions. Most importantly, they realized how all of this is important to building a future-based, successful business. This doesn't mean that they had instant success--it just meant that they knew who they were and what they had to do.

Discussed, Negotiated and Agreed Upon

There are a few ways that values and guiding principles should be used in the strategic, tactical and operational planning process:

> **First**, they are used in ground planning the foundational beliefs of the company.

> **Second**, they are reviewed to ensure that any decisions made are in line with what the company is about.

> **Third,** they are used by the business leaders and senior management team to enable the organization's culture.

Without these three actions, it will be impossible to fully engage your stakeholders. Also, the business leader and management will need to make sure that the values and guiding principles are all mutually agreed upon and everyone has full buy-in. That's why collaboration in creating and/or revisiting them is so important. If your values and guiding principles no longer fit or work for your business, it could be that they were created in isolation. That is, someone sat in a room, looked up a bunch of values and guiding principles, copied them, wordsmithed them a little, brought them to a meeting, showed them around, said they were a good idea and suddenly you have values and guiding principles for your business. Your stakeholders will consider these bogus and totally full of fluff.

True values and guiding principles are discussed, negotiated and agreed upon. They get supported. The stakeholders in your business are educated and will quickly see any disconnect. So don't insult them by providing them something that they can't believe in. Make sure your values and guiding principles are lived, used and supported. You will do a lot better as a team-based organization if you do.

Finally, when constructing your values and guiding principles, try and follow that golden rule: keep it simple. Way too many organizations make them complex, and when that happens, no one remembers them and your stakeholders lose interest or don't care. Don't make that mistake. To keep them simple, a good rule to follow is to have no more than five key values and five guiding principles. Make sure each is well defined and easy to explain. Also, make sure they are not generic, but real to you and your stakeholders. Trust me, your stakeholders will know the difference!

Values and Guiding Principles Guidelines

First, start with a checklist of values. This exercise is designed to help you reach a better understanding of the most significant values of your business. Select the most important as a guide for how your business is supposed to behave. As part of this first step you'll need to identify a smaller list. For example, if you had a list of fifty potential values you would first focus on only selecting ten, and then on only selecting five. It's always best to have only five core business values. Also, make sure you create a list that people will believe and remember. This is harder than you think!

Second, define exactly what your values mean. That is correct—you and your team must decide each value's definition as it relates to your business. They must connect and make sense. Often the entire team discusses each value and determines the meaning. If your team gets stuck in this step, use the posted note method. Get each person to write out a couple of points as the definition, place it on a big white board and then work together to create the best wording for that value. Don't look up the meaning in a dictionary or someone's book. If you do that then no one owns it, and accordingly, no one will use it.

Third, test your values and guiding principles. Use a form of scenario-based planning, business problems or opportunities to test them out. Discuss in what way each value and guiding principle applies to the situation being discussed. The key is to be able to make business decisions at different organizational levels using your values and guiding principles. If you can make decisions that make sense and keep what you believe intact, then your values and guiding principles are sound.

Stick with Your Parameters

It's a Test

With the mining resource company mentioned earlier, there is an interesting sub-story of values and guiding principle impact. A potential business partner and client approached the president of the resource company. In order to win that business, the resource company had to agree to give a little to get a lot. In other words, pay for the business through a combination of bonus payments.

The president of the resource company chose to take the high road and declined the offered opportunity based on the fact that he wanted to ensure he supported his company's values and guiding principles. If the president had accepted the offer he would be going against their value of business integrity. It turned out that by sticking to their values and guiding principles, the company—his company—ended up getting awarded a different project that provided substantial reward for the company and its stakeholders. They passed an external litmus test.

Go or No Go

Values and guiding principles will inform you whether you should make a business deal or not. They become the yard (meter) stick that you must consider in the decision-making process. Being able to connect with a vendor or possible business opportunity beyond financial return is a concern for many companies around the world. This is especially true for companies with values that support green thinking, community health or ethical behaviour. Granted, companies have to make money—that's the way the world works. But business leaders with integrity know that they need to connect with like-minded people and organizations that share a common set of values and guiding principles. This is the only way to stay true to who you are.

Making short term decisions, the "just for now" choices, cannot last long. Eventually chaos will ensue and many holes will appear that will eventually rock your boat. Planning and the decision-making processes are meant to help the leadership team deal with both short-term and long-term issues. This means they are anchored in your vales and guiding principles.

If you follow a true set of values and guiding principles and connect them with your vision and mission, there should be times where the business leadership is willing to walk away from a business arrangement or deal. Your values and guiding principles should be part of that business decision process that enables business leadership to be clear as to the way they will manage the business. They should keep you in check and be something that you do not want to compromise.

Parameter Set

Working with your values and guiding principles will keep the business leadership and your project teams within certain parameters. When it comes to stakeholders, it's all eyes on the leadership team and whether they walk their talk. By building a set of values and guiding principles that the leadership team can truly support, it frees the team to provide the leadership that key stakeholders are looking for. And honestly, it's much easier to work in a principle-based environment.

Employees Need to Know

People need to know that there are guidelines, a set of parameters, a sense of reliability about their workplace. They need to know that the leadership team supports and embraces what the company is about. They need to know that the values and guiding principles are true. They know this through how they are treated and the level of respect they are shown. Business leaders who truly believe in the company will engage their employees using the values and guiding principles. They will share stories of how they make decisions and will encourage others to do the same. Values and guiding principles are for everyone in your business. People and culture get developed through engagement. The true sign of engagement is when your people establish a sense of themselves.

Final Thoughts

If you don't have explicit values and guiding principles, then it's imperative that you take the time to create them. If you do have them, re-visit them and determine if the values and guiding principles you have today still hold for tomorrow. Make sure they are simple, easy to understand, and compelling enough that everyone in your business can buy into them. And finally, make sure that your senior management team (as well as your entire organization) lives by them.

7

Goals and Objectives

The goal is not to do business with everybody who needs what you have. The goal is to do business with people who believe what you believe.
– Simon Sinek

A Little Pensiveness Goes a Long Way

We have things we need to achieve, places we need to go and people we need to see. Yet nothing gets done unless we take the time to think about just exactly what needs to get done and why. That's the core of strategic planning: developing or rethinking high level goals and objectives so that the organization, the teams and individuals all have something to work towards, a common end point, a common direction.

Vision – Mission – Values – Principles	Goals - Objectives

Just like there are three main levels of organization, there are also three main levels to goals and objectives: the strategic, the tactical, and the operational. As was stated in Chapter 3, *The strategic is about the what and why, the tactical is about the how, who, and when, and the operational is about the here and now.*

Strategic goals and objectives are long term and require a specific level of thinking.

Tactical goals and objectives are mid-range (perhaps within a year or two) and may end up being projects that we need to complete within a specific timeframe. They have a clear beginning, middle and end.

Operational goals and objectives, on the other hand, are short in duration—they could be hourly, daily, weekly or, at most, monthly.

Every business can be divided into these three distinct levels of goals and objectives.

In the Long Term

In strategic planning, your team will need to stay focused on the long-term agenda of your organization. Long-term goals and objectives are for the whole company. They are over-arching and determine what the company should accomplish and where it wants to go. They give the business leadership and the senior management team focused intent.

Mid-range goals and objectives will come afterwards and serve as the translation of the strategic goals and objectives into actionable work. They'll be focused on the tactical stakeholders: the mid-level manager, the project manager, team leaders, supervisors, etc. Only then do you get to the short-term goals and objectives. These are for the foot soldiers--the people in the field representing your business and making a difference to your customers and clients.

In order to play a successful game, these all need to be strongly linked together, and for this to happen, the leadership team needs to get clear on what the long-term strategic goals and objectives are and what is on the strategic agenda for the organization.

Keep your Eye on the Ball

Assuming that you're working with the S.E.T. Approach, by now you've decided upon who should be involved in the planning process, developed and/or audited your vision and mission, achieved clarity on your values and guiding principles, and you've had some futuristic thinking and discussion around what it is you want to achieve in the next three, five, ten, fifteen, twenty years or more. With all of this accomplished, you should now be ready to establish your long-term goals and objectives.

In strategic planning, these are often referred to as strategic agenda Items. They arise out of the work that was done establishing your benchmarks and assessing your business environment. Since you're looking into the future, you're not looking for perfection at this point—the fine-tuning will come later. If you're using the SET-Ability model as your planning guideline, this is the time to decide on the high level goals you want to achieve over a set period of time.

Finding Your Vision of Success

I recently asked an audience in a strategic planning workshop, "Where do you see your business 25 years from now?" Surprisingly, many had trouble answering the question. Yet when I asked them where they see themselves in retirement, they had no challenge at all. Most could tell me exactly what they saw for their lives in the future.

When it comes to setting goals and objectives, imagine yourself in retirement. You are 25 years young and you are thinking about your retirement in 30 years. That would make you 55 years old. At the heart of financial planning is a personal strategic plan. In that personal strategic plan you would have a vision of success and goals and objectives that have been met. The goals and objectives come from your vision of success. Often the things that you say you've accomplished will provide the language for your high-level goals and objectives.

The Long Game – Sports and in Business

If we bring this to the football field, the short-term goals and objectives are to move the ball along the field and make a touchdown. Yet there is a lot that goes into making that touch down--everything from having the right people on the field at the right time, to the execution of key plans and strategies, to fulfilling long-term goals and objectives. For many teams, it's about winning the Grey Cup or Super Bowl—something that may take one or more seasons to accomplish. To get there takes time and a lot of forethought. Somewhere along the way, a plan was put into action. That plan had long-term goals and objectives.

Sports are a good example, as they are well represented in the media and by various sports associations. If you listen to the dialogue, there is a lot of talk about the long-term game plan. The business leaders, senior management team, players and all the other stakeholders need to be on the same page for things to work. They need to know what it is they are out to achieve and what their over-arching goals and objectives are. Neither sport teams nor business teams are created in a day.

Test Your Team

One way to test your team is to place a blank piece of 8.5 X 11 piece of paper on the table in your boardroom with a well-sharpened pencil beside it. When your senior management team sits down, ask them to write down what the five strategic goals and objectives of the organization are and why they are important. When presented with this quiz most of the team will fail to be able to articulate and answer the question correctly.

If this happens to your team, it either means that the strategic goals and objectives are not well-developed and defined, they are out of line with your reality, have not been ingrained in the leadership psyche, have not been listened to, and/or have been forgotten. The dialogue afterwards is the most important, as it forces the planning team to discuss or re-discuss the strategic agenda items and what they need to accomplish. Keeping the goals and objectives front and center while bridging the gap between the strategic and the tactical/operational will make you most successful.

Focus on the Road Ahead

A Truck Full of Grain or a Fleet?

Focusing on the road ahead can be boiled down to the 'what' and 'why' of the business. It's what strategy is all about. The foot soldier is about the tactical world and ensuring things get done. Just like the foot soldier has their eye on the details, the CEO has their eye on the bigger picture. Where the foot soldier is concerned about loading a truck full of grain or repairing a belt elevator, the business leader is considering buying a fleet of trucks to give the overall company a competitive advantage. That bigger picture must have clearly stated strategic goals and objectives that the team can work towards. This cannot happen unless the business leadership and management team are on the same page and can answer the question, "What is on the strategic agenda of the organization?"

Some of you reading this section may think, "Well that's obvious! Of course that's where people on the different levels should focus." But it's not what always happens. There are many examples in business were the CEO/President is focused on operational issues and where the operational resources interfere with the larger business objectives. Clarity of roles and focus is important.

Round and Round We Go

Establishing the strategic goals and objectives for your business isn't always easy for a senior management team to do on their own. They often have too much on their plate in the day-to-day world, drawing their attention away from high-level planning. If you find that your team is getting stuck in the details of the discussion (i.e. thinking tactically) and things are going round and round in circles, consider hiring a professional facilitator. An outside facilitator can help the senior team to focus their efforts while remaining independent and neutral to the outcomes. They can also help in the setting of goals and objectives and bring you through a road map process, freeing your team to focus on the strategic level and not get distracted by operational details.

A Structure to Follow – Be SMART

Ultimately, long-term goals and objectives should be written down, shared and passed on. To help you achieve this, consider using the SMART structure:

S   Specific - specific, not general

M   Measurable - able to be measured and verified

A   Attainable - achievable within reasonable limits

R   Relevant - worth doing in the context of your organization

T   Time bound - specific dates or duration[15]

Examples:

- Build a $75 million dollar company in 3 years while focusing on an EBIDTA of 15 percent
- Enhance our corporate culture through a stabilized and engaged workforce with a turnover rate of no more than 5 percent in 3 years
- Enhance our business processes for efficiency and effectiveness contributing to positive bottom-line impact and cost savings of 15 percent
- Improved operational efficiencies resulting in a cost of doing business of 85% of revenue in 3 years

The SMART principle for creating goals and objectives can be used as a litmus test at all levels in the organization. Always start with what is on the strategic agenda and from there, make sure they link at each level of the organization: the strategic, the tactical and the operational. For each goal and objective simply ask yourself, "Is this statement SMART?"

Focus and Intent to Win

In a game we want to score and we want to win. We do so with focus and intent. The game is like mid-range goals and objectives that need to be achieved in order to play in the bigger events. Not just in the finals, but for the cup, the final prize. In the mining service and health service companies discussed earlier, there was an emphasis placed on understanding the vision and mission, the values and guiding principles. For the same reason, there needs to be an emphasis on clarifying your long term goals and objectives of the business. It's not just about game day; it's about the long haul and what your people need to do and focus on to get you where you want to go.

If your strategic agenda items are set, then your people can focus on the key initiatives for your business. These are the enterprise or business programs that need to be invested in for the long term. The best way to handle key initiatives in your business is to ensure that your senior management team identifies programs they can connect back to the items on your strategic agenda. This will help you ensure that you are creating linkage between your strategic agenda items and your key initiatives—your programs.

It is these strategic agenda items and the identification of the key initiatives that will guide all the additional work that needs to be done in your company. If your people don't know what is on the agenda of your organization, they will make a lot of mistakes. They will do a lot of things that don't need to happen, jumping down rabbit holes that will not support where your company is going. As a business leader and as a management team, you will spend a lot of time putting out fires and you will not achieve your vision overall. That's just the way it is. To win, get clear and get focused.

Making a Connection

Once your planning team has solidified its strategic goals and objectives and articulated them clearly, the next step is to make sure they're recorded and communicated appropriately. Your internal stakeholders need to know what is on the strategic agenda and why . This way they can translate it into actual tactical and operational work. You need to make a connection with your foot soldier, the people that will do the work. They, too, need to understand the strategic agenda items (high level goals and objectives) and the key initiatives (the enterprise and program work to be done). It is your people who will help you create implementation plans and successfully execute them to bring your future to life.

Final Thoughts

Many people don't recognize the importance of having a set direction that everyone knows and moves in alignment with. They think "Oh gee, another 'Goals and Objective' discussion." One of the best statements I've ever heard from a CEO was the acknowledgement that, after going haphazardly through 15 years of business, it was good to finally have focus. Lesson learned. Get focused now, develop your high-level strategic goals and objectives, and stop going down rabbit holes. Be SMART. Be SET for Success.

PART FOUR

Focus on Your Key Business Impact Zones

"See the ripple effects you create. It's all in the actions you take."
– Richard Lannon

8

Process and Productivity

Productivity is never an accident. It is always the result of a commitment to excellence, intelligent planning, and focused effort.
– Paul J. Meyer

The Way We Do Our Work

Process and Productivity
(the way we do our work)

We lead very busy lives, but are we being efficient and effective? That is what the business impact zone of process and productivity is all about. Process and productivity is about the way we do our work and how we get things done. As a business, the way your organization does its work is important. Efficient and effective organizations can better compete in the world at large and give much more satisfaction to all of the stakeholders, both internal and external. In the strategic planning process, it's imperative that the impact zone of process and productivity tie back to the mission, vision, values, guiding principles, and strategic goals and objectives of the business.

As a business, you are either efficient and effective, or you are not. If you're reading this book, it's quite likely that there are things in your business environment you'd like to see work more smoothly, more efficiently. There are many reasons for poor processes and less productive business environments, ranging from lack of clarity on the part of the business leadership and senior management to performance management system structure and the way people are rewarded to poorly implemented initiatives to business leaders who micro-manage (not letting people under them do their thing and make decisions). Any one of these can be affecting your process and productivity.

One helpful way of looking at process and productivity is in terms of Kaizen opportunities. Kaizen refers to a philosophy or practice that focuses upon continuous improvement of working practices, personal efficiency, etc. When applied to the workplace, Kaizen involves all employees (from the CEO to assembly line workers) and refers to activities that continually improve all functions. It also applies to processes such as purchasing and logistics, which usually cross organizational boundaries. By improving standardized activities and processes, Kaizen aims to eliminate waste, thereby making your business more productive. And, as the Kaizen approach seeks to improve processes, productivity then is the yardstick by which you can measure your success.

Move with Precision

Every business enterprise should be looking strategically at being lean, with consideration for their existing process levels and their process maturity levels. In the movie *Dances with Wolves*, John Dunbar, the main character, describes the buffalo hunt. In particular, there is a narrative section where he mentions that he'd witnessed no other group of people who could move with military precision, using only what was needed and wasting very little.

You see, John Dunbar was a military man on a journey that brought him to the Lakota people. He learned many things about himself and about a very different group of people and the way they were organized. He learned this through interaction with the leaders and the people, through dialogue, through the celebrations, and through drawings that depicted their processes, their way of life, their travel and hunting patterns and the way they were efficient and effective at what they did and how they lived. Not only is *Dances with Wolves* a great movie, it is also a great study in organizational structure and the importance of process and productivity. In a way, it was like a study in being lean and the Kaizen opportunities needed to be productive.

Generally Kaizen looks at waste in some key categories with Seven Lean Approaches. These include:

1. Waste of Motion
2. Waste of Waiting
3. Waste in Transportation
4. Waste in Storage
5. Waste in Defects
6. Waste in Processing
7. Waste in Over Production[16]

The Military has to Move

Believe it or not, most of business thinking in process and productivity is grounded in the military—in lean thinking and finding Kaizen opportunities. The military needs to move large groups of people, fast. They need to consider all aspects of process—time, distance, yields, stops, decision points, intersections and connections with other processes.

A MASH unit (Mobile Army Surgical Hospital) is the epitome of needing to be efficient and effective. They're there to serve and support the men and women on the combat field. People's lives are at stake. Every part of a MASH unit has a process and following that process is the key to their success or failure, to whether lives are saved or lost. They have no choice but to run a lean environment with a consideration for allowable cost and productivity. Their mandate is to save lives under what are often extreme circumstances. To do so they must operate with well-designed processes. Their measurement of success is simple: lives saved.

A Thought for Health Care

There are many ways of approaching lean thinking in your business. One way is to create more efficient processes. This can be seen in the healthcare industry, where there is a revolution taking place about lean thinking. One example comes to mind in radiology, where it took 51 days to process a radiology request. There were many holding patterns along the way, with the request often getting into someone's drop box and sitting there for days. Imagine if you could get that down to 18 days. It doesn't sound like a huge improvement, but it is. The teams start processing paper faster with less lag time. Imagine the impact if you could improve a process by 66%!

Most businesses say they do not have enough time, money or resources; process and productivity improvements are meant to free up these constraints and contribute positively to business impact. In this specific case, the hospital in question would serve its clients better through trimming the unnecessary steps and holding patterns and moving patient requests more quickly. In essence, eliminating the "waste of waiting."

Leave it to the Automobile

Henry Ford had a deep understanding of process and productivity, particularly on the manufacturing floor level for his first car, the model T Ford. He understood the line from input to process to output. That's why he's considered the forefather of the manufacturing line of mass production. Get the product done and out, productively, and at a low cost. In the time of Henry Ford, you could have any colour car you wanted—as long as it was black. You see, black dried faster. Modern manufacturing is more complex, particularly given the rules of business and the expectations of product quality, yet in the end the same economic principles apply.

Your Maturity Level is Important

Every organization, be it a group of people, a community, a military unit, a government body, a manufacturing company or service company, is at a different level of maturity when it comes to process and productivity. There are maturity process levels that exist in every business, just as there is a need to be lean. It's all part of the natural business evolution. Every business and department evolves along certain maturity levels either organically or intentionally. It's also common to become stuck in one place along the maturity continuum.

To begin the strategic planning around this impact zone, your team will need to assess your business's level of maturity. Consider these five evolution maturity levels:

- **Chaotic**: no real structure – everything is at the 11th hour
- **Reactive:** all last minute – plan is open – when the leadership says jump, the team says how high
- **Proactive:** repeatable processes in place – managing efficiency, but not business needs
- **Service:** semi-integrated processes – able to measure business economics
- **Value:** connected processes – measured and shared[17]

What is your business maturity level, not only for the organization as a whole, but also its various departments? What are all your business processes? In what way does your maturity process level(s) impact your business productivity? What level of maturity do you want to be at (or need to be at)? By when can you achieve that maturity level? These questions will help you determine your present business process maturity level(s) and your future desired maturity state. They create dialogue among your people on what improvements need to be made and the commitment it will take to make them happen. Once you've thoroughly explored these questions, add into the conversation the need to be a lean business environment, one where value for the end customer is considered and you now have a recipe to recreate your business process and production practice.

Process Impacts the Organization

The Enterprise Initiative

There are many different types of strategic process initiatives that can cut across the entire organization. These are often referred to as enterprise initiatives and usually claim the biggest bang for the buck. They're part of the enterprise's commitment to do something new that will benefit the whole organization, whether it be decreasing costs, improving productivity, or finding ways to increase market share. It might be that your organization's accounting or human resource system—be it paper or technological--has run its course and your company cannot operate within the parameters of the existing system. If that's true, the SET-Ability factor of that system (process) will need to be looked at. It's time for the business to consider the best way to fine-tune its operations to achieve the best, most consistent results that are going to positively impact the organization.

The Organization Structure

Maybe your organization has matured or grown to the point that your current structure is no longer adequate for business needs, either now or in the future. This could be a sign that it is time for an organizational restructure. Savvy companies don't restructure their structures for today, they restructure for where they want to be and what they want to become.

Another element of business organization falls under human resources. If your business is struggling with the way work is getting done, then maybe it needs to look at its people processes. People processes are sometimes the first place a business needs restructuring. The key here is that you identify the need for change—you see where your business processes are lacking in efficiency and make the needed changes.

Process Re-Engineering

It's possible that your business has grown from a few people to lots of people, whether through sales growth, organic growth or acquisition. It's also possible that things have gone the opposite direction and you need to do more with less. Whatever the means of change, process re-engineering might be your focus.

Business Process Re-engineering (BPR) consists of rethinking and radically redesigning an organization's existing resources. BPR, however, is more than just business improving; it's an approach for redesigning the way work is done to better support the organization's vision and mission. Re-engineering starts with a high-level assessment or review of the organization's mission, strategic goals and customer needs. Basic questions are asked, such as

- Does our mission need to be redefined?
- Are our strategic goals aligned with our mission?
- Who are our customers?

An organization may find that it's operating on questionable assumptions, particularly in terms of the wants and needs of its customers. Only after the organization rethinks what it should be doing, does it go on to decide how best to do it. So BPR is very strategic, with tactical and operational impacts.

There are a number of common reasons why business process re-engineering is done. Some examples include:

- to maintain your competitive advantage
- to mitigate the downside of a major enterprise systems implementation
- to adhere to industry best practices and business rules

- to improve market integration of products and services
- to avoid the trap of doing things the way they've always been done
- to address rapid growth issues that have forced you to change the way you work
- to address changes in laws that are forcing you to do things differently
- to avoid trouble that is on the horizon
- to change in senior management team
- to address customer base dissatisfaction with the company's output
- to create a better more stable working environment for your people
- to address technological advancement in the industry

The point is that something is driving the need for change and you are either on the bus when it comes to re-engineering your business, or not.

It is all about the Way We Do Our Work

Athletes have a process for preparation for an upcoming event, whether they're competing individually or as a member of a team. Chances are, they follow a routine that was pre-planned and execute it with precision. Maybe it was a process that would take them from a middleweight to a heavy weight ranking in their sport. Or maybe as a swimmer they always came in second, but with a new coach, a new approach, a keen focus and the development of a winning routine they go beyond and become number one. They followed a process—a productivity process. Great business leaders do the same thing.

Experts Can Free Up Leaders

At the senior levels, a business leader's efficiency and effectiveness is directly tied into the form of engagement they have with experts. These experts, whether they're a part of the process or are subject matter experts, free the business leader up to focus on the over-arching business, the enterprise as a whole. A great way to illustrate this is through the marshmallow challenge.

The Marshmallow Challenge

The Marshmallow Challenge was invented by Peter Skillman of Palm, Inc. and popularized by Tom Wujec of Autodesk. The key to this challenge is to have a team build the tallest structure in 20 minutes using 20 strands of spaghetti, one yard of tape, one yard of string and a marshmallow.[18]

The results are very interesting. Business leaders do well, but business leaders working with an assistant do extremely well. Why? As a team, the business leaders and their assistant are better together. The assistant is an expert in organization, in keeping things together and moving things forward. They take on the role of the 'expert' in the process of getting things done. In the business world, they'll be the ones that understand all of the in's and out's of how the system works and can ensure that things get done in a timely manner, freeing up business leaders to do what they do best: lead. That creates efficiency and effectiveness for the business. This applies to your teams as well. Let them be experts in the right processes.

Buckets of Work - Levels

Everything that happens in your organization and cuts across the levels of organization can be divided into 'big buckets' of things that the business does. Chances are, you have some people in charge of those buckets. Often we see human resource, financial, information technology, and manufacturing processes being part of the list. But what if your organization has other things going on? You might have a whole research and development department that has processes that cut across the organization. If you missed these in the high level identification of business processes, you might create negative impact for the company by not representing all the true processes that exist.

There is an impact to understanding that all organizations can be broken down into at least a four level process model like the maturity model used earlier in this chapter. However, there are other process level models that look at the business slightly differently. Tari Kaupapa from the project office of Massey University outlined a Four Level Process in his paper on "Process Mapping; Process & Guide." He used the following guidelines to understand and identify the different processes in the business organization:

> **Level One:** is the standard high level and lists the operational levels of an organization.
>
> **Level Two:** depicts the end-to-end processes across the operational areas.
>
> **Level Three:** shows the roles and associated steps required to complete a specific process within an operational area.
>
> **Level Four:** is the documentation of instructions and procedures required to complete steps in the level three processes.[19]

Within this model everything must link and connect. Failing to do so could have bottom line impacts, due to cost changes and productivity mishaps. It's also important to know exactly which level of the organization we are dealing with and when. The candid discussion happens when you review your business process maturity levels at the same time as determining what process level from Kaupapa's model you are at. The best bet is to pick your processes and then figure out with your team what process levels you're at, which buckets they belong in, how they link together and where improvements need to be made.

Level 2 and 3 are the tactical levels in this model. You'll need this level information, both for strategic conversation and also to bridge the gap between the strategic and the operational. Whatever happens, level 2 and 3 in your business should be categorized and be part of the level one items--those big buckets that have impact on the entire organization. Level 4 thinking is in the weeds and is not for the business leader. Still, it is often customer-facing and is therefore important for you to know and understand, especially around how it impacts to your business. Awareness is what is important here.

Final Thoughts

Every business I have ever worked with says that they are unique and unlike any other business. Yet every business has the same three constraints – not enough time, money or resources. Being more efficient and effective is imperative if you are going to deal with these common business constraints. One of the ways to do so is to address your business processes and productivity.

9
Tools and Technology

I think it's fair to say that personal computers have become the most empowering tool we've ever created. They're tools of communication, they're tools of creativity, and they can be shaped by their user.
– Bill Gates

What we Use to Do Our Work

> # Tools and Technology
> (the tools we use to do our work)

Tools and technology go deeper than just computers, communications, and the transfer of information. They are the very fabric of our economy. When they don't work, there is negative business impact. They are part of every business decision and they exist everywhere. They are strategic enablers. You have an alarm clock to wake you up, another device to monitor your heart, a smart phone to link in with people all the time; you drive a car, take planes, pass by fleets of trucks, dry your hands with a hand dryer in a public washroom, and much, much more. We live and breathe by the very nature of the things that we've created to do things in our every day lives and in business. Yet these tools and technology are only a means, not an end. They're meant to help us achieve the things that we work at every day, not substitute for the end goal.

As much as they can be helpful, our tools and technology can also be the source of what seems like catastrophic stress. A major social network goes down (Google, Facebook, Twitter, LinkedIn, etc.) and we can no longer work. A system fails and we freak out. It's a crazy, mixed-up world when what helps you get things done can also stop you from working. Have you ever arrived at work on a Monday morning going about your normal routine--you turn on your computer, go get coffee, come back to your desk, log in--and then nothing works? Who hasn't experienced a minor or major computer glitch that stopped us from working?

Maybe you work as a mechanic and the air-compressed tools are aging. One day you arrive at work and prepare to repair your first customer's vehicle, only to discover that a necessary tool has failed. Suddenly everything stops. The bottom line is that there is business impact. Your business may be down for a while as you find a work-around, repair, or replacement for a key part of your workflow. The point? Your tools and technology are a major impact zone that needs to be considered carefully.

Technology Gets You to Where you Need to Go

Flying with the Airlines
Former Westjet President and CEO, Clive Beddoe, was noted for commuting on his own company's planes. He would introduce himself to the various people and at the end of the flight, get

up and thank all the passengers who flew on Westjet. Clive also liked to talk about his airline.

On one occasion, he engaged me in a discussion about the strategic decision to retrofit WestJet's fleet of planes with more aerodynamic windows. By doing so, the planes expended less energy and saved fuel. At the time, it was a hard decision for the business leadership team to make. Spending money on tools and technology is often a serious capital investment and forking out the money—even during economically favourable conditions— can be a difficult decision. At the time, fuel prices were on the rise and Clive's company had some difficult decisions to make. Retrofitting an airline with aerodynamic, streamlined glass was a capital investment in the future that would contribute positively to the environment and the business, yet committing to that level of cost wasn't something that the senior management could take lightly. It took a while, but eventually the decision went through.

Clive was happy with senior management team's leadership, foresight, and decision to make the investment. It not only helped the company in the long-term, it also turned out positive for a number of important stakeholders.

Keep On Truckin'

Years ago I had the opportunity to work with the president of a major truck manufacturing company. This company provided both individual and fleet options to customers who need reliable, commercial trucking options. They were a profitable, respected, world-class custom builder of trucks, as well as a distributor of parts to the heavy-duty aftermarket resource transportation industry. They provided tough trucks for tough jobs. I was asked to find out the purchasing decision criteria of their primary customers: trucking companies.

A trucking company can consist of everything from a customer who is a single owner-operator with only one truck (which they often live out of and work from) to a large enterprise comprised of entire fleets of trucks. The vehicles get well used, wear out and have to be replaced as they age. As a large trucking company, you would need to be continually looking into either reinvesting in your current vehicles, buying new vehicles, or perhaps even considering the purchase of an entire fleet of new vehicles. The replacement of your fleet is an example of an investment in tools and technology that will allow you to perform at your best with the latest and newest equipment. It can be a difficult capital investment decision, as replacing large trucks is expensive and a major commitment, but if your current fleet was aging and needing constant repair, a fleet of new trucks may just be the investment needed to take your business to the next level.

We discovered that trucking companies who had bought from the manufacturing and distribution company had a number of criteria for their trucks when it came to toughness, reliability, comfort, low maintenance, improved fuel efficiency and customer service. Otherwise stated, their clients had specific business requirements for their decision, particularly as this was a capital investment into the tools of their trade. The trucking companies took their investment decisions seriously, and lots of consideration went into the purchase. No differently than an airline who is considering upgrading airplane windows. Usually the vendor that won the work and got the order could provide some form of advantage in an extremely competitive environment.

Understanding the tools and technology your clients use will better enable you to provide something of value, something that solves their challenges when it comes to getting work done. My client, the manufacturing firm, was able to use this information to tailor their product to their customers needs. A win for everyone.

Technology Refresh

In the technology world, companies will often need to do a "technology refresh," an upscaling to newer technologies in order to meet the changing needs of the business. In today's fast-paced world, tools of the trade often become obsolete, particularly in the hardware and software world where it's common for vendors to cease supporting a specific software or hardware platform. Needless to say, this can have a major impact on a business. On a personal level, suddenly your favourite application or hardware toy will be no longer available; on a company-wide level it could mean no more forward or future-looking movement for your current systems. An external force has put your business into a situation of changing your present tools and technology, and usually that means it's time to upgrade. Strategically, business leaders need to determine when is the best time to do a technology refresh, as technology refreshes generally impact many, many aspects of your business. If not done correctly, it can bring your business to a screeching halt and have a high cost in wasted time, money and resources.

Create a Competitive Advantage

Combination of Attributes

One of the primary reasons to invest in tools and technology is that they can create a competitive advantage, making them a strategy enabler. Competitive advantage occurs when an organization acquires or develops an attribute or combination of attributes that allow it to outperform its competitors. New technologies such as airplane windows, a fleet of trucks (lowering fuel and maintenance costs) or information technology (software and hardware) can provide that competitive advantage, whether as a part of the product itself, as an advantage to the making of the product, or as a competitive aid in the overall business process. Either way, it can make the business more productive and more competitive. In the planning process, common goals for tool and technology enhancement might include:

- enhanced systems and business processes to better enable product and service delivery
- building strong IT knowledge needed to support systems
- developing a scalable and cohesive business technology system that improves human resource services (payroll, vacation, etc.)
- investing in new technologies that enable financial department
- establishing systems access, procedures, templates and cheat sheets.

Construction - A Disconnect Impacts Everyone

Sometimes there can be a strong disconnect between a business initiative and a technical solution, and this can have a profound impact on an organization and its stakeholders. For example, there are many companies that have manual customer service processes that work well, but sometimes it's imperative that the system be automated. That is a serious investment in technology.

One such example happened in a construction materials distribution company. Their billing system needed to be updated from a manual system to an automated one. When the system did not produce expected results, blame-storming occurred, particularly as the business people said that the technology department was at fault. A quick review of the facts showed that the business leadership and management team had never showed up for the enterprise-wide systems discussions.

The impact was felt not only interpersonally and interdepartmentally, but also in the cash flow of the company. Billings were not going out and money was not coming in. Another issue appeared where orders were not being filled in time and that caused the customers to be negatively impacted as well.

A Lesson for Everyone

What went wrong in the picture above? Not everyone had been fully engaged when the upgrades were on the table. In order to decide to install new windows on a fleet of planes, purchase a new fleet of trucks or refresh a technology, business leaders need to be aware of the requirements and be fully engaged.

Just like the strategic planning process where it's important that the right people are at the table, the right people need to be engaged in discussions around tools and technology and subsequent business investments. If the right people aren't involved, the business will not get what it needs. The result? Per the example above, blame-storming and other departments—like the technology department—become the scapegoat for business strategic agenda items gone astray. In addition, the business and the technology departments miss out on the opportunity to become strategic partners. The bottom line? Key stakeholders need to be fully engaged when investing in the things we use to get work done.

Leading Edge or Bleeding Edge

As you no doubt already know, there is real impact when it comes to investment in tools and technology. Sometimes immediate and other times not. It can often be a balancing act of being on the leading edge or the bleeding edge.

Being on the leading edge is like being on the front edge of something that is moving. It's part of being on the most important or most advanced area of activity in your field. Finding the cure for cancer would put you on the leading edge, and this leading edge would generally provide you a sustained competitive advantage as long as it is timed well.

On the other hand, the bleeding edge suggests that everything is so new that you could have a high risk of failure. The bleeding edge will cost you time, money and resources with the potential for significant losses. They key is to be able to determine which edge you need to be on. Sometimes innovation means you have to go a little further and take a bit more risk and that could put you on the bleeding edge. Either way it is a tough choice to make.

Is it Needed?

Before considering a tools and technology upgrade, you'll need to understand the customer's needs. Countless companies invest in tools and technology that customers do not want. They miss the opportunity to discover the voice of the customer in the process of wanting to upgrade. Take the lone wolf CEO who spends a million dollars on a piece of high-end portable manufacturing equipment for oil and gas drilling companies, only to discover that he was ahead in his thinking and the customer was not interested in buying these particular drilling tools and technology. It was a nice piece of equipment, but it was not what the customer needed. We can take a lesson from Henry Ford who understood what customers needed: they wanted faster horses, but what they needed was reliable transportation. I wasn't around when that was quoted, but it sure applies today!

A Change is Coming - Succession

In western society, business organizations are bracing for a major change. Over the next 10 years, 200,000 small business owners in Canada alone will turn 65 and in the USA it is estimated that 250,000 American small business owners turn 65 and want to retire. These numbers don't include their employees, mid-to-large businesses, corporations and public organizations. When you add all of those together, this clearly becomes a critical issue with major impacts and ramifications.[20]

One of the areas that businesses continue to explore is the use of tools and technology as a means to mitigate the need for additional people. It is an automation of the workforce in ways that we can hardly even imagine. With this succession come decisions around the use of tools and technology, and what you will invest in. New tools and technology will be needed to accommodate your business succession challenges and the ever-changing economic playing field.

Making the Connection

There is a clear linkage between the impact zones of tools and technology and process and productivity. These are often referred to as the "hard side" of the business within the SET-Ability model and have everything to do with the way your organization is structured. That is, in part, why we say, "Structure your approach to your business." A linkage must be drawn from the vision, mission, values, guiding principles, and the strategic goals and objectives with consideration for process and productivity and tools and technology. It is the connection between the way you do your work and the tools you use to get things done. Make sure you make that connection.

Final Thoughts

When you are looking at your tools and technology make sure you consider your process and productivity as an interconnected player in your decision-making. These two impact zones play off each other, creating business impact.

10

Business Development

In marketing I've seen only one strategy that can't miss - and that is to market to your best customers first, your best prospects second and the rest of the world last.
– John Romero

The way we get our work

┌───┐
│   │
│   Business   │
│   Development   │
│   (the way we get our work)   │
│   │
└───┘

As you can imagine, business development is a major impact zone for companies of every size. From the solo-preneur and small business owner to the non-profit organization, government agency and major corporation, without business development there would be nothing to do.

Business development is the way we get our work. It's a key impact zone for all organizations, public or private. If your company needs to secure opportunities, funds and resources either internally or externally, you are involved in business development. To put it another way, business development consists of the approaches taken to create and implement growth opportunities.

When it comes to strategic or program planning, business development is one of the important impact zones and a key pathway to business success. It's often at the top of the agenda and creates opportunities for everything else. In today's world, the choices for business development are endless: social media, traditional media, growth through acquisition, moving into a market and setting up shop, building a strong business development network, etc. If this impact zone is not carefully thought out and executed with precision, there may be no tomorrow. Here the old adage wholes true: nothing happens unless you create a sale. This means creating business development opportunities.

Expanding Opportunities

Often we think of business development in terms of for-profit organizations, as they are generally focused in profit and/or strategic directions. In these cases the dialogue will be focused on actions the organization must take to maintain their present state or to expand into other markets. Some forms of expansion include:

- focusing efforts on sales and marketing
- acquiring other companies
- linking key supply chain elements
- building partnerships and complementary alliances
- creating organic growth opportunities

These are just some examples of the many approaches a business enterprise can take to build market share, advance its vision and mission of success, and achieve its goals and objectives.

Many Ways to Build a Business

More than a Hole in the Ground

There are many options for business development at the strategic and program levels. For example, a mining service company might elect to build its business through geographic expansion and focused organic growth of its service delivery. They would increase their output by either expanding their customer base or introducing/developing new products. In the case of one particular mining company this was done through situating its technology and services next to their customers, an obvious thing to do if you're providing a product to large, corporate mines where time, cost and quality are important criteria for the customer. Here, geographic location is everything.

Partnerships and Alliances

As part of the organic approach to business development, you may decide to partner with other stakeholders in a given geographic area to ensure your business can expand into that marketplace. This could include local citizens, government, special interest groups, investors, or in this case, maybe even the mine itself. There are many examples where the customer has partnered and invested in a technology-based, service-driven company to secure their supply of a product or service they required.

Healthcare Getting into the Act

Another example is that of a public hospital engaged in the three pillars of service: public health, research and development, and patient care. If they choose to engage in business development in order to secure funding for research and development, their business development approach must align with their strategic goals and objectives.

Efforts might be placed on government funding, grant development, academic liaison and special interest group involvement. This makes for a very politically sensitive landscape that the senior business leaders must navigate in order to ensure the hospital is meeting its strategic mandate. As part of the business development impact zone, the hospital must ensure that it considers all facets of its business development approach and how those link back to the greater mission, vision, goals and objectives.

A Non-Profit Situation

Even though most non-profit organizations prefer to focus on board development, management, fundraising, and polices in their strategic planning efforts, many of them must also seek funds to stay in business. Once this happens, they're stepping firmly into the arena of business development. Seeking funding, pursuing grants, and offering fundraising events (i.e. hosting an annual gala, having silent auctions, donation campaigns, membership's fees, event meeting fees, training programs, etc.) all fall into this important impact zone, and like the other top impact zones, all actions taken need to be firmly grounded in the mission, vision, goals, and objectives.

A Service Provider

Other ways of moving forward in the business development arena include expanding one's existing footprint, markets, product, and service offerings (through offering additional services to existing customers).

Recently, a technology service provider decided to do just that. They'd recognized that their technology product was really not going to change much—that it had reached the apex of its maturity—and that future changes would only happen if the industry were turned on its head due to some huge innovation, which they believed unlikely. Therefore, in order to meet its strategic goals and objectives, focus had to be on organic growth and expanding the existing footprint. It became the way to build the business and is an accessible approach that most small-to-large business owners can engage in.

The key is that there needs to be a service and product plan in place, and that the offerings are complementary and make sense to the customers and the other stakeholders. With organic plans focus is on business growth through increased output, existing customer enhancement or expansion, or new product or service development.

Finding Your Approach

Having the right dialogue with your key stakeholders (including your business champions and top management) is imperative when it comes to business development initiatives. It's another aspect of having the right people to talk to. Dialogue should be focused on getting very clear on where your work comes from.

Making Sales

Nothing else happens in your organization until you make a sale. Regardless of whether you're a for-profit or a non-profit organization, your funding has to come from somewhere. It's what drives our world. And since markets expand and contract based on many factors, business organizations are often getting squeezed from a number of different directions. It's no different than your householder needing income to maintain a certain lifestyle choice. You need to make the money and you need to spend the money.

In the end, it comes down to knowing what it is you want to achieve and then making the investment to make it happen. **Business development drives the business world**. Without business development you won't be doing business. The other key impact zones will become irrelevant unless you have a means to getting sales (i.e. income).

Marketing Considerations

Marketing can help you drive sales opportunities. It's the process of figuring out the value of a service or product and using various ways to provide information and communicate with potential customers. There are **ten primary marketing components** that help create business development opportunities. Chances are, out of the ten marketing options, three are your key marketing drivers and one brings in the most business opportunities. Your options for marketing include:

1. **Phone Calls:** Getting on the phone and connecting with your potential and/or your existing customers. Most businesses have some form of "phone them and make it happen" approach.

2. **Direct Marketing:** Connecting directly with your ideal customer is an ideal situation. Direct marketing can be achieved in a number of ways--traditionally through print media, and today through email and social media.

3. **Advertising:** Generally considered traditional in terms of prints, radio and television. But now, with social media, you can blend your approach or focus on a single media. Advertising itself, though, is generally considered a one-way communication approach.

4. **Publicity and Public Relations:** Works well for getting free media and is important. Free media, whether traditional or not, provides your business credibility. It's always good to get it and use it properly. Media outlets, whether traditional or not, are looking for a story and content. Give it to them.

5. **Networking:** This is a broad category that includes engaging people at special events, business events or in public locations that share a common interest, etc. The key to networking is that you attend events that are unique gathering places for your potential business clientele. Otherwise it's a waste of your resources.

6. **Presentations and Public Events:** These are used to create community and business recognition. They are important opportunities that build societal confidence in your marketplace, your company and its people. Or maybe it helps you build your business. Either way, business leaders and professionals should build these skills and consider public speaking as a valuable business exposure opportunity.

7. **Advocates and Fans:** This is all about the people that support your business and have influence with your customers and clientele. Every business that interacts with external or internal customers should develop advocates and communicate with them regularly.

8. **Tradeshows:** Trade shows are central to the business development agenda of a number of companies. They're a great opportunity to connect with customers and gain market share. Tradeshows are particularly important when introducing new products or services.

9. **Enhanced Information:** This is a powerful tool for business development and often requires the selection and implementation of a customer relationship management system (CRM).

10. **Partnerships and/or Complementary Alliances:** A partnership should be a legal arrangement with another firm for the purpose of joining forces and serving a particular clientele. A complementary alliance, on the other hand, is a more informal arrangement where two organizations share resources and offer complementary services to a shared clientele.

11. **Follow Up Program:** It might sound like common sense, but a lot of businesses do not have a well-defined follow up process or system that truly lets them stay connected to their present customers and warm leads. This is a must in today's business world and should be a key initiative.

10-3-1 or 80/20; It's all in the Numbers

There is a general rule that says for every ten business development opportunities, three will be a possibility and one will stick—the old **10-3-1 rule**. That is ten calls, three meetings, one sale. There is also the **80/20 rule**. Now if my memory serves me from my days studying economics in university, the 80/20 rule was named after the Vilfredo Pareto by Joseph Juran. He applied the Pareto rule to quality issues. For example, 80 percent of the problems were caused by 20 percent of the issues.

Applying this thinking to economics we can say 80 percent of income was received by 20 percent of the population. So we must assume that most results in a situation are created by a smaller number of causes. This would mean in the case of your business, 80 percent of your work comes from 20 percent of your efforts or clients. Using the 80/20 rule and looking at your present revenue stream might provide insights as to where you should direct your focus.

Because effective business development relies on knowing where your sales and revenue comes from, you might want to consider an audit to understand the linkage between revenue and business development initiatives. This discussion should be focused on what you need to invest in that is going to create growth opportunities. It's part of knowing your numbers.

Business Development Plans

Every business needs a business plan--a formal document of the business's goals, the reason you want to attain them, and the way you're going to make it happen. This is an important piece, because often people confuse business plans with strategic plans. Granted, they may be interchangeable at times, but they're not necessarily the same thing. Strategic planning is for business leaders and their teams to get focused on the key impact zones of their business and align them with the strategic agenda of the organization. It is an enterprise plan. Once that is done an over-arching business plan is often created, a strategic initiative that the business leaders must engage in to ensure that they can achieve the things that they say they want to achieve.

Thought on Champions – Business Champions

When you start to discuss business development someone has to own it, especially when an overarching business plan is part of the key initiatives. Business champions are individuals that go beyond their operative responsibilities. They are individuals trying to influence strategic issues larger than their own immediate operational responsibilities. They take the *initiative* and accept responsibility and accountability for it.

Business champions in your organization are imperative to your success. If you are a solopreneur or a corporate CEO, having champions around you builds the organization's success. The potential ways and objectives of championing cover the whole process of strategy, from the formation of the content to the process of implementing these contents. "Champion" can be used more specifically to refer to a senior manager who champions the project, ensures that it is properly resourced, and uses their influence to overcome barriers. In this case, we're referring to business development champions: people who have their eye on the ball and know what they need to do to ensure the success of the organization. Someone has to own it.

Figuring it all Out

Get Your People Involved

As with any impact zone, you need to get input from your people. This could be your other managers and/or the senior management team, senior professionals, and even your external stakeholders. You could even consider input from your front line resources. Granted, they will be detailed, but their input goes a long way towards building internal trust.

One thing to be careful of, however, is ensuring that the people involved understand that this is not about sales and marketing tactics directly, but rather about connecting to what the business wants to achieve and what they will need to focus on to achieve it. The discussion should be focused on specific business development initiatives that are linked to other aspects of the business. General options should be discussed. Maybe it is growth through acquisition, or growth through organic means, or growth through geographic expansion, or even growth through frontline activity. It all depends on the needs of your business.

Connecting with Your Strategic Agenda

All business development initiatives need to be tied back to the strategic goals and objectives of the business, either at an enterprise level or at a program level. At the enterprise level, one of the common strategic goals and objectives to which business development is linked is sustained financial success, particular to a specific time frame and providing a good bottom line return – usually in revenue or cited as a percentage. Examples include:

- establishing technology home services growth of $25 million with a before tax profit of 15 percent
- building a $100 million dollar company in 3 years while focusing on an EBITDA of 17.5 percent
- generating an average annual net income of $5 million over the next 3 years and annually achieving a 15% return on equity

These are some of the possible strategic agenda items that can get you and your team talking about what needs to happen to make it happen. The end result is often a combination of organic growth, mergers and acquisition, enhanced sales force development, or some combination of business development, tool changes or process improvements.

Linking Key Initiatives

There can be any number of initiatives and programs that a company can establish to maintain their organization and/or use for expansion and growth. In fact, just about any strategic item can be turned into an initiative or an overarching business program. For example, the third item above—establishing technology home service growth of $25 million in three years with before tax profit of 15 percent—might require a number of focused initiatives. Examples include:

- focused growth through geographic business expansion (locally, regionally, internationally)
- focused growth through organic initiatives using our existing approach to business
- focused growth through strategic acquisitions (buying the competition or partnerships)
- enhanced sales through new hires and training to drive sales and build business value
- established value added products and services for our marketplace
- developed fund raising initiatives that expand supporter reach and funds
- find investment and funding acquisition for future business growth

Some of these items may or may not contribute to achieving the overarching strategic agenda item above. A discussion must be had and decisions must be made as to what is realistic. And as with any strategic agenda or initiative item that is associated with an impact zone, it is important that these initiatives are SMART and connect directly with other impact zones, especially since each key initiative may have several streams of work associated with it.

Assign a Resource

To make sure your business development succeeds, someone will have to own it. If your business development is about strategic growth and advancement, then the CEO and President needs to own it. If it's about organic growth, maybe a VP or Director owns it. The business leadership team ensures they maintain responsibility and are accountable to the organization. If it's about driving sales force enhancement, it's conceivable that a senior professional or manager can own it, but there would have to be a solid business leader associated with it for coaching and mentorship. Without that, you and they may fail. This is not necessarily about position—it's more about the best resource you have and doing the best with what you have.

Some Common Sense

Every strategic plan I've ever done (actually every enterprise program or project plan I've ever done) has started with business development in one way or another. Whether I helped facilitate the process, or the plan was already created and given to me as a business artefact, business development was always at the top of the list. It's almost always the first item on the strategic agenda, which is no surprise as, in the end, it's what drives the business.

There are serious consequences to every business or organization that relies on creating sales or establishing funding if the business development does not come first. It sounds like common sense, but there are many examples where a new leader was more focused on process and control, and therefore missed opportunities to invest in growth. With smaller companies it can start with a technical team that gets contracts, but does nothing to maintain or grow their market, usually because they're too busy to fulfill that roll. These companies often find themselves in trouble in a declining market.

It's best to apply common sense and put your business development first.

Final Thoughts

As part of your planning approach, business development is a transforming component that has the potential to create a massive business impact. As mentioned earlier, **nothing happens unless you create a sale.** This means creating opportunity, whether by picking up the phone or placing your business next to the customer so that they will come in for a buy. It will all depend on what you want to accomplish, what key initiatives you're going to focus on, what the buckets of work will be, and by when you can have them done.

11
People and Culture

Employees are a company's greatest asset - they're your competitive advantage. You want to attract and retain the best; provide them with encouragement, stimulus, and make them feel that they are an integral part of the company's mission.
– Anne M. Mulcahy

The Place We Do Our Work

People and Culture
(the place we do our work)

One common element on the strategic agenda often concerns the investment you plan to make in your people and the culture of the organization as a whole. People need very specific things in place for them to do their work well and be individually satisfied.

The Soft Benefit

There are many benefits of understanding the people and culture aspect of your business. Granted, they are considered "soft" benefits, but efforts are being made to create realistic measurements to understand the actual business impact of people within organizations.

In planning and team development, it's essential for the business leaders and the senior management team to understand not only whom they're working with, but also each individual's business impact. By understanding some key components of your people, you can design your organization appropriately and make clear choices as to where different individuals fit. When people fit their work, companies report fewer sick days and productivity goes up.

People

In the workplace, it's important to have the right people with the appropriate skills, the right level of experience, and the ability to learn. Every business has to keep up with the breakneck speed of change in their field, and the ability to learn and be adaptable is now paramount to success.

Culture

The culture of an organization is about its beliefs, values and attitude. Every individual in your business has a set of beliefs and values, and an attitude that encompasses them. What we're looking for here is whether or not these beliefs, values, and attitude are appropriate for your business.

In the absence of strong leadership, clear direction, guidance, and structure, your people will create their own culture. It's far better for the leadership to set the tone for the culture and create a place where people want to work, rather than letting things run their own course.

Ultimately, as a business leader, you need to create a culture where people are all rowing in the same direction. This is achieved through establishing an understanding of self and others, developing people's skills and abilities (both hard and soft), and working with them as a team to achieve the organization's objectives.

The People and Culture Mix

People and teams should be challenged and have the opportunity to develop the right skills and experience. In addition, they should also be able to apply their aptitude and align themselves to a set of beliefs and values they agree with. This will allow for a positive attitude to prevail throughout the organization, which will in turn create positive business impact and make a difference for your company, customers and the larger business community. It's up to you—the business leaders and management team—to make this happen.

Everybody Fits Somewhere

Understanding the people and culture element is an essential part of any business initiative, whether it's strategic planning, project planning or business analysis. Sometimes you just need to know who should be part of the planning process, how people will interact, and what their business impact will be. Other times it's about understanding the natural tendencies of an individual, how best to work with them, communicate with them, coach and mentor them.

A Change in Attitude

An oil and gas service company rich in technology and clientele grew rapidly. They went from 1 to 100 people in 3 years with millions of dollars in revenue. That rapid growth created issues, from business processes to people challenges. This is a common experience in rapid growth situations. There is often a combination of issues that move between the process and people impact zones.

In this case the organization experienced increased conflict due to a lot of leadership and people changes. As time went on, these became further elevated. People felt as if they didn't know what they were supposed to do and to whom to report. The business leaders understood that this was an issue that needed to be solved and took it on as part of their strategic planning process. They decided to profile the top 25 business leaders, managers and key senior professionals in their company to establish a clearer picture of the interactions among the teams and where improvements could be made.

Some of these changes were in the area of roles and responsibilities. For example, there was a sales person who was struggling to make their targets. They were a little reserved, focused on details, had excellent analytical skills, and yet was challenged in their attitude. In the past they'd made some excellent sales and everyone thought they should therefore be in the sales department. Upon further discussion and organization analysis, however, it was decided to move them to the Quality Assurance group. This was a big change, but that person could then take on a team lead role. It did mean some skill upgrading and certain certifications were required, but today they enjoy the work they're doing. Not only does it get them out of the office and into the field, they still get to speak to customers as a subject matter expert and deal with the information that they love. They are still brought in on sales that require focused analysis and attention to detail, but in general, their focus is on quality assurance. Once they began doing what they enjoyed, their attitude totally changed.

Insight Makes a Difference

There was another employee in the same company—a senior professional--who was asked to join in on the profiling. They were noted for their ability to solve any problem in the field that the company and clients could throw at them. This made them a highly successful and creative technical professional who made a difference for the company. In essence, they were the go-to person to solve major technical problems.

During a business impact session this subject matter expert had some personal insight. They realized that they didn't want to be part of the larger strategic planning process and that they'd prefer to stay focused on what they did best—being part of a smaller field team that creates positive business results through their technical expertise. Not everyone is meant to be involved in planning, but that doesn't mean they can't make an important contribution. In this case, the professional understood their impact and where they could provide the best value.

Successful Technical Professionals

Often companies make mistakes with their highly successful technical professionals. They seek to involve them in programs that are not their natural inclination or seek to promote them into senior leadership roles, primarily because they are so successful at what they do and their customers love them. Yet this is not always the best thing to do, either for that particular individual or for the organization. In this case, the senior professional understood both where they wanted to be and where they needed to be. They were glad to participate in all programs where they could provide their expertise, but recognized that they needed to stay where they were if they were going to continue to have positive business impact.

Where People Fit

Not everyone is meant to be a leader or they are meant to lead something else. In this case we could be addressing the senior professional, the supervisor, the manager, team lead, or senior manager. I've had many discussions with CEO's who had a team where one or two people didn't quite fit into their present 'leadership' role. It's not that they were bad people, but their natural tendencies led them in a different direction.

Years ago I witnessed a personnel restructuring of a major automobile company. One of the fellows I worked with, a leader, was moved from a senior leadership position in sales to being head of the parts department. This person was not happy with the move—they felt it was a demotion.

One day I entered the elevator with the president of the company. We were alone, so I asked why he'd moved this person into a position they were not happy about. Graciously, he looked at me and said, "That is an inappropriate question, but you are young so I will answer it. You see, people have natural abilities. The person you admire is a better fit to lead the parts department. They may not know it yet, but they will do amazing things. Just wait. You will see." Interestingly enough, he was right. The new parts department lead found he had a natural ability to make that department exceed performance expectations. I know—I transferred into that department to be part of its success.

Everybody fits somewhere. They will particularly excel if their natural tendencies are leveraged. As part of personnel dynamics we must understand people and their culture, and be supportive of who they are. That is the right thing to do.

Understanding Others

In the second example above, it took a while for the business leaders to understand why someone would not want to be promoted beyond their present role. They just assumed that promotion was something everyone would want. Yet the personal needs, goals and objectives of the individual don't always align with promotion. They need to be in a role where they can succeed. Often the best person to make those decisions is the individual themselves. In this case, the senior professional understood their strengths and knew where they could lead and have a more profound impact. They requested a different role than what was being offered. In the end, the business leader granted them their preferred role and responsibilities. It takes a real business leader to understand where their people fit best and then place them there.

Knowing Where People Fit

It is important to appreciate the differences in your team and know how your people think, work, and fit into the bigger picture. Some are strategic, some are tactical and others are purely operational. Every organization needs a balance of different types of people.

Strategic or Tactical Thinkers

From a planning perspective, we need to know whether a person is a tactical and/or a strategic thinker, their strengths and weaknesses, and the impact they have on the business. Strategic thinkers tend to naturally gravitate towards "what and why" and tend towards long-term thinking and impact. Tactical thinkers focus more on the "how, who and by when." If you can understand where your people fit in terms of their thinking, you can design a planning and implementation program that leverages them.

Tactical Teams Bring Implementation

As mentioned before, tactical thinking is the thinking of the project teams, the technical professionals and experts, and the mid-management. Your tactical teams know how to get things done. They help define the implementation process for your initiatives. They become responsible for outcomes and that makes them the doers. This applies throughout the organization.

Attitude Impacts

People bring a lot to the table in planning sessions. They not only bring their natural tendencies, they also bring their culture—complete with their own beliefs, values and attitudes. There is an old joke that illustrates how one person's attitude impacts another person:

An employee arrives at work.
The Team Lead asks, "Employee, how are you today?"
Employee replies, "I'm not sure. Is my boss in yet?"

This story illustrates that the employee is unsure of what their day will be like, because they do not know the mood or attitude their boss will be in that day. In this case, the boss's attitude or personal whim that day impacts the attitude of their management team and, therefore, the employees.

Are you that boss or team lead or project manager?
What impact do you have on your people?

Your approach to people and culture is important. It impacts the level of success you can achieve in your business.

Profiling Your Organization

Profiling your organization can help you understand the people and culture of your business. It's similar to the audit/strategic assessment, but is focused on your people instead. You can use assessments to better understand a person's fit within a team and your organization, hopefully providing you with a more objective synopsis of a person's strengths, weaknesses, working style and areas for growth. Often benefits sighted for profiling include:

- expanded self-knowledge: response to conflict, motivation, stress; problem solving ability
- embraced a more adaptive style that allows you to get along better with others
- enhanced constructive and creative group interactions
- improved better teamwork and less team conflict
- refined and stronger sales skills as a result of identifying and responding to customer styles
- established the ability to manage more effectively by understanding the dispositions and priorities of employees and team members
- improved and better impact regarding productivity and the bottom line

Understanding Self, Others and the Organization

There are some common profiling tools used within organizations to help the management understand people and teams and the way they fit together. What individuals do and why they do it is important for your whole team to understand, especially prior to strategic planning or rearranging teams. Business team profiles, debriefs, and impact sessions can provide leaders with insight into their natural inclinations, the way they impact their peers, their decision-making processes, and the actions they will take. These assessments are useful in understanding if you have the right people in the right places, thereby helping your team and business rise to the next level. Here are some examples of profiling tools:

- Myers Briggs Type Indicator
- DISC Profile
- Birkman Method
- Career Anchors
- Keirsey Temperament Sorter
- Work Preference Indicator
- Self Management Pro

These profiling tools can help you assess your teams and the individual natural abilities. Whether you want to understand how people work together, where people best fit or you want them to understand one another better. Each tool listed above has a different focus, so to decide among them consider what it is you want to accomplish and then apply the best tool for the job.

Understanding people allows the business leader to address whether you (or a team member) are the best person to engage. These are often very difficult decisions to make, but if you are taking an honest look at your organization you need to understand where people fit.

Short Term Understanding

On a smaller scale, profiling helps the facilitator and business leaders determine the best fit for the planning cycles. It will also help tactical teams better understand how they should work together. There is a positive impact to individual and teams understanding self and others in the context of the work that needs to be done, especially when it is work that will have a profound impact on the business's future success.

Longer Term Impact

For longer duration initiatives, organizational reviews help forge decisions around structure and personnel development programming. People and culture is an important impact zone, and their training and development needs must be addressed, particularly in an organization that is grown on the backs of technology, technical professionals and/or a service-driven environment. Other programming deals with talent management initiatives. This is especially important today as we brace for a work resource shift due to retirements. Efforts should become focused on a more adaptable work environment. That is a big change.

Create a Place for People

Every client I've worked with wants to have a place where people actually want to work. As part of your planning, you need to find those strategic agenda items that will forward your intentions for building an organization where people want to work. Examples might include:

- enhancing the corporate culture through a stabilized and engaged workforce
- investing in our culture through continuous learning and personnel development

Often organizations build programs and initiate projects around the following kinds of statements, mostly talented management programs. For example:

- develop a comprehensive talent management and human resource system
- create and implement a performance management approach
- establish recruitment, retention and loyalty programs for our organization
- create an employee communication plan to ensure better connection with our people
- establish management and staff training & development programs to include workshops, coaching and other types of professional development programs

These should be based on the fact that you have profiled your teams and have taken into consideration your present performance concerns and personnel development requirements.

Understanding people and culture has to do with benchmarking, it is that 'line in the sand' we talked about before. On one side is where you are and where you were. (The where you were is what got you to where you are today.) On the other side is where you want to go and grow. All successful planning truly requires the participants to baseline themselves through a people-and-culture profile and the creation of a talent management approach.

People Need Structure

The reality is you need a plan. A plan that addresses not only the more concrete key business impact zones (process and productivity, tools and technology, business development, etc.), but also addresses the people and culture in your business. What are you are doing today and tomorrow to embrace building a highly effective work force for the future? As part of the planning process, structure always comes up and people spend a lot of time playing with their organizational and team structures. There is a reason for this: they are looking for the best structure to solve their business problems today. What if you planned for the future structure? What if you could put a structure in place that you can grow into, one that is future-reaching and addresses the future needs of the organization? People need structure, and teams need to know how things fit today and tomorrow. It's important to see the future of your business and how you can benefit the organization over all. Often missed is the people and culture element, mostly because it is considered a soft cost with no hard returns.

A Message for You

The people and culture you work in are extremely important. Most organizations know this, but many merely talk the talk without walking the walk. They're not in sync with what they believe. I recall a family member who worked at a company where their leaders said one thing, but then treated their people differently. The company had over a 30 percent annual turnover rate. I don't know any organization that can maintain corporate integrity and profitability with that level of turnover. Focus needs to be on the investment in your greatest resource—your people—to truly create and maintain a successful organization. **Believe it or not, people have a choice. You need to treat them well.**

Final Thoughts

Successful businesses have demonstrated that when you have the right people doing the right jobs, a future-facing structure, and a culture that people can embrace, there is a strong positive business impact.

Build it and they will fulfill it.

12

Measurements and the Financials

In many spheres of human endeavor, from science to business to education to economic policy, good decisions depend on good measurement.
– Ben Bernanke

The Way We Know We Did Good Work

Measurements are essential for understanding what is happening in your business--what gets measured gets done. In a business environment, measurements come in many forms and include hard, soft, lagging and leading indicators.

Measurable Outcomes   (the way we know we did good work)

Lagging

Lagging indicators are used to measure performance and allow the leadership team to track how things are going. Because output (performance) is always easier to measure by assessing whether your goals were achieved, lagging indicators are backward-focused or "trailing"—they measure performance already captured. Just about anything you wish to monitor will have lagging indicators.

Leading

Leading indicators are precursors to the direction something is going. For instance, changes in building permits may affect the housing market, an increase in new business orders could lead to increased production, interest rate changes will impact spending and investments, a decrease in demands for natural resources will often indicate work slowdowns, and an aging population may indicate future stresses on the healthcare system. **Because leading indicators come before a trend, they are considered business drivers**. Identifying specific, focused leading indicators should be a part of each business's strategic planning and decision-making process.

Hard vs. Soft

Hard measurements might include the investment required for a building, a truck, or a computer. These can be considered capital expenditures. Soft measurements, on the other hand, might include time saved through the use of a new technology. Taken all together, we tend to call these measurements key performance indicators (KPI). In your planning and decision-making process, you'll need to discuss and identify your business measurements, what they mean, and the impact they have. The primary challenge is determining the correct measurements for your business.

Telling the Business a Story

It's in the Bag

There are many ways to consider your business measurements or key performance indicators (KPI). The most important thing is that they tell you something important about your business and the industry you are in. For example, a retail cement company that provides instant concrete in bags to big box hardware stores might consider the number of consumer bags packed, placed on a palette, put on trucks and shipped to customers per day as a key performance indicator. This measurement reported daily is a lagging indicator: it is work done in the past that helps the management team know whether a business unit was performing to its capacity on a given day and the potential profit that day. The format of this measurement could be units packed per person per day (u/p/p) or units shipped per day (us/d).

The point is that there is a means to measure production and the impact it has on the bottom line for the business. As such, the staff and the management need to know what type of measurement suits the indicator best, monitor the work, and then review the measurements to know how well they are doing.

Patient Turnover

A hospital, on the other hand, would have a different set of measurements. They might consider inpatient and outpatient flow as an important KPI. The bed turnover rate gives the number of patients using one bed in a time span of a year. This can further be calculated into a facilities cost per bed. This would allow planners to understand outpatient flow and areas for potential improvement.

Rooms for Rent

Hotels and motels also monitor check-ins and check-outs. They know their vacancy rate. For example, the operational cost of a room might be fifty dollars a night , with a retail rate of one hundred and fifty dollars a night. If they can't sell a room at their full retail rate, it's better for them to get one hundred dollars for a room than nothing at all. So the room goes on sale.

Someone has calculated the cost of doing business and the impact of having a vacant room. They know that having a room filled is better than having an empty room. More importantly, they can monitor room activity and determine what they should do to ensure that the hotel is full. They also know that money will be made in the extras that people buy. The value a customer brings is understood as a lifetime value (LTV): the value that the customer has over the course of their hotel or motel usage life and the amount of money someone will spend on average at a given location. It is far better to know your measurements and be able to make informed decisions than to just lose money.

Back to Boundaries

As mentioned in previous chapters, it's important to know where your boundaries should be and set them accordingly. This is important, as you are either inside or outside of your boundaries; you are either on one side of the line of the other. You need to know exactly what your numbers are so you can make key business decisions and know the improvements you need to make in relation to your ideal boundaries. Sometimes it is just a matter of making adjustments within the boundaries that already exist; sometimes you'll need to readjust your boundaries. Either way it, you need to know where you are. In the SET-Ability model, each impact zone represents a category that requires boundaries with numbers that directly relate to it.

Process and Productivity

Productivity is a measurement—it measures your workflow and processes. In what way are you productive? Are you making your numbers? What if you work in an organization where a customer comes in, you submit a request, and it ends up in someone's in-box for three days? Now imagine they responded and forwarded it to someone else and the original request sat in another in-box for three more days? We would consider that a very inefficient and ineffective process. You need to understand how work flows through your organization; measurements for process and productivity allow you to do that.

There are many productivity measurements for goods and services produced, including physical and financial value. Examples include sales produced, standing inventory cost, labour costs (full time equivalent), time and speed lapse, value added, etc. Often productivity is measured in terms of an equation: productivity = output/input. Where there is a relationship between the quantity of output and input to create output. It is basically a measure of the efficiency and effectiveness of your organisation in generating output with the resources available. It's important that you keep your eye on the numbers here, as productivity is critical for the long-term competitiveness and profitability of all businesses.

Tools and Technology

Tools and technology are the enablers within your business. They permit your business to become successful through the skilful application of either automation or people. As a strategic enabler, that application of tools and technology will ripple throughout the organization and your business impact zones. If you don't have the appropriate tools or technology, you won't be able to effectively complete the work. The investments in your tools and technology and their effective use need to be measured to ensure that you are getting all that you can out of the tools of your trade. You need to know exactly what's in the inventory and how much money you need to invest in order to upgrade. Then you make the adjustments that need to be made, including the approach you're going to take to realize the hard costs over time.

Business Development

The same thing holds true in business development. It is an investment in the sustainability and/or growth of your business. Some measurements might include:

- increased customer acquisition for products and services measured through repeat customers
- increased market penetration measured through percentage of potential markets acquiring a service
- calculated and tracking a customer's life time value and worth over time
- established of suppliers' stability measured through connection with delivery and revenue
- improved market share penetration measured by percentage of market ownership
- enhanced customer Life Time Value – that is the value a customer has to your business over a period of time
- understanding of cost per lead and cost per sale per customer

When it comes to business development, you need to make sure that there is a return on your investment. Savvy organizations are finding ways of establishing campaigns, creating partnerships, and/or acquiring services rights that have direct measurements associated with them. Whatever approach you take, you'll want to know your return. Finding the best ways to measure it will help you make better decisions and see the path you need to take.

People and Culture

Measurements can also help the leadership team better understand the impact your people and culture are having on your business. Although measuring the soft components of a business may sound like trying to catch the wind, soft costs can be determined through careful study. There are also some measurements that can help:

- employee turnover rates
- sick days and absenteeism
- leadership and management complaints
- employee litigation
- time saved on work activities
- skills capability gap analysis for employees

Putting programs in place to help stabilize the people environment, create a culture of satisfaction and build your people abilities will also make a strong difference. Often companies will focus on things like educating their people in proper tool use and workplace safety, communications and conflict management skills, and developing team cohesiveness. Creating a prosperous culture has a lot to do with good leadership, a willingness to be innovative and inclusive, and a wiliness to let go. Look to your talent to find ways of creating a better culture. They can also help you determine the measurement you need to put in place to better understand your business environment.

Common Financial Measurements

There are many financial measurements that businesses use to understand their performance. If you are looking to determine if a particular approach or initiative is a good idea, it's important to use some of the more common measurement calculations. Commonly used financial measurements that you should know include:

- Quick Ratio
- Current Ratio
- Return on Assets
- Inventory Turnover
- Receivable Ratios
- Net Profit Margin
- Debt to equity

Other common financial analysis calculations can help determine either the lagging (in the past) or the leading (in the future) impact of a decision. Here are standards that every business leader and professional should know and understand:

- Breakeven Analysis
- Sensitivity Analysis
- Return on Investment
- Profitability Analysis
- Net Present Value (NPV)
- Internal Rate of Return (IRR)

There are many others, but in the final analysis most businesses focus only on a handful of potential calculations to determine if something is a good idea or not. If you're responsible for business solutions recommendations, then the financial measures listed above are the ones you need to know. I always recommend to business leaders that they train their teams on understanding numbers and what they mean. This holds especially true for the tactical professionals who have to research and recommend solutions to business problems. Hopefully, the senior management team already understands the numbers and knows how to interpret them. If they don't, it will have a negative impact on your business.

Impact Zone Decisions

To decide on where to invest, you'll need to take into consideration all the key impact zones and think about what will best forward the success of your business and your people. You'll also need to consider your business constraints (time, money and resources) and your business drivers (the things that are vital to your organization success). Identifying your leading and lagging indicators will help you make decisions on all of these areas of consideration.

Get Outside Your Comfort Zone

Though there are some guidelines that can be used, there is no "one" way to define the key performance indicators for any particular business. They are as unique as your approach to strategic planning and decision-making.

Present Knowledge

You need to start with what you know and can already measure. Most businesses are already measuring their bottom line or cash flow, be it positive or negative. They may also be trending their sales track or monitoring their turnover rate. Either way, cash flow or other known measurements is a place you can start.

Outside Your Comfort Zones

One thing that's often critical at this stage is to step outside your comfort zone. Go outside your senior management team and get additional leadership and external business stakeholders involved. Stakeholders go beyond your internal teams. An outside perspective can often help you determine what your lagging and leading indicators are, as well as help in recognizing the key leading indicators for your market—those measurements that will drive your business. By involving external stakeholders, you are involving what is important to your customers or investors. Among other things, this helps you avoid wearing rose coloured glasses. It's way too easy to be blinded by our own thinking as to what a good measurement is. Others can help.

Back to Lagging

The next thing to consider is whether your current indicators are what you should be measuring. These will be lagging indicators, i.e. things that you have done in the past. Just be aware, you're taking a historical survey of where your business is at, not a future look. What has happened in the past can be a great place to discuss the future, but it is not necessarily what will happen in the future.

Always keep an eye on your lagging indicators--they will continue to provide insight into your business. Poor lagging indicators generally translate into poor leading indicators. A performance indicator survey—a benchmarking tool that provides data so you can better understand your present state of your business—might assist you in the process of ensuring whether the indicators you are using are appropriate. It is designed to facilitate benchmarking and peer group comparisons. The challenge is to ensure you have the correct indicators, and that your management team understands how they can be used to align your business impact zones.

Choosing Leading Indicators

Choose your leading indicators carefully. For example, we all know we have an aging population called the baby boomers. These people are supposed to have disposable income and potentially many health issues. Hospitals, fitness and other health organizations are asking in what way they can tap into this aging demographic. Or maybe your leading indicators include interest rates, debt ratios and housing starts. Increased building permits can be a leading indicator for designers and other people in similar professions. The leading indicators should be unique to your business environment, originate from your key strategic initiatives and work elements, and ultimately be used to drive your business. Try not to be too ambitious. Keep focused on the business key impact zones represented in your strategic plan.

Train the Management Team

Train your leadership team to understand the key indicators and how to use them to improve the business. We tend to assume both that we're measuring the right thing and that people understand what the numbers truly mean (i.e. they understand the impact) without really checking in to see if that's the case. It's important that your team can not only identify the measurements, but also recognize the potential business impact indicated by them.

Getting it Correct

Not every business gets their leading or lagging measurements correct. There are lots of examples of businesses that missed the trends. The buggy whip manufacturer missed the importance of the automobile, encyclopaedias missed the importance of the CD, and the internet and automobile manufacturers, if not careful, will miss the challenge of the decline in finite natural resources and the importance of alternative fuel options for an educated consumer and the natural limitation of any system. Fast food companies will miss the importance of good help and experience a societal backlash against their products and services. Missed trends and opportunities carry with it repercussions. Only through watching your leading indicators can you best determine the trends and business drivers for your business's future. This requires that you look at larger global happenings and translate them into national, regional and local requirements.

Final Thoughts

In order to make better business decisions, you need to have the right measurements across all of your key impact zones. Ensuring that you have the correct indicators may be a challenge, but it's vital to the ongoing health of your business. Make sure your team's strategic planning process includes determining your indicators and that everyone understands what they are and why they are important. **Remember, what gets measured gets done.**

Know your numbers.

PART FIVE

Plan It - Map It - Implement It!
Go the Distance.

13

The Strategic Map

I use doodling for a variety of reasons: I use it to get clarity around a concept, I use it to relax, I use it to communicate ideas with others and get their refinement of them, I use it to map complex systems for companies, I use it to run innovation games for business, I use it to get insight on something puzzling me.
– Sunni Brown

The Visual of all Your Key Business Decisions

We've outlined the planning and analysis, as well as the model and process. Now it's time to put it all together by building a strategy map. A strategy map is a graphical representation of all the key business decisions that have been made using the S.E.T. Approach and the SET-Ability model. It's generally used to bring all of the pieces together.

Linking the Key Impact Zones

Represented Information

Your first item of business is to make sure you have documented all of the business requirements you and your team have identified as important. All parts of the SET-Ability model are represented on the map, including

- vision and mission
- values and guiding principles,
- goals and objectives,
- process and productivity,
- tools and technology,
- business development,
- people and culture, and
- measurements

Each impact zone is a way of categorizing all the moving parts of your organization. Your business measurements will be outlined for each impact zone, regardless of whether they are leading or lagging indicators. Before you get started, however, you'll need to decide the documentation format that best suits the needs of your business.

Crisp Dialogue

It's also important to have a crisp dialogue with your senior people. That is, a candid discussion about focus and what is truly important. They need to be engaged in the process as representatives and contributing members to the decision-making process. They need to visually see those decisions so they can be communicated clearly. Going the extra mile, converging all the information, and making decisions is ultimately what planning is all about. Building a strategy map gives you the blue print to bring your business to its next level. It's the vetting of information that counts. This process can also be used for tactical and operational purposes, as well as for other levels of business that require matrixes and maps.

Pulling it Together

In order to have your business running on all cylinders, there must be a place for all the key business decisions and focus areas to be captured. No matter where you are in your business life cycle or your business size, everything needs to get pulled together somewhere. The place to pull them all together is a strategy map, a document where you can see all of your decisions and provide a visual of everything in one place.

Information Integration

Building a strategy map is an important part of integrating the decisions you make in the planning process into your business as a whole.

Cross Business Units and Departments

The process of integrating information will often yield discoveries—opportunities that you can leverage. For example, when the Chief Information Officer (CIO) of the oil and gas company recognized that the business had three separate Information Technology Departments spread across three geographic territories, we identified it as an opportunity to bring these departments together so that they were all on the same page.

Each business unit shared similarities and were part of the energy section, yet had distinct responsibilities. Even so, there was enough commonality in the business units' IT infrastructure that they could share services and resources. If they did not share services, the company would continue to diverge, negatively impacting its productivity, cost and resource requirements. They determined that the merger of their IT departments would create an economy of scale -- decrease costs, increase productivity, and leverage resources.

The strategy map provided a one page visual where the department leaders put all of the pieces together, saw where they needed to make changes, and then made key business decisions about how to accomplish these changes effectively.

Keeping Things Standing

Using a strategy map can help all sizes of organizations. Take, for example, a 35-year-old, mid-range commercial building service provider that needed to get clear on their strategic plan requirements and the future direction of their company. With a head office in Western Canada and branch offices in all the major business centres throughout the country, the company needed to focus its efforts on what they would be doing in the next five years to continue to be successful. The business had matured and had not kept up-to-date on their strategic initiatives.

After revisiting their mission, vision, impact zones and measurable outcomes, they realized that they needed to focus on key items including organic and acquisition growth, succession planning, enterprise technology integration, and process changes. They developed a strategy map using all of the impact zones and tied everything back to the overall strategic goals and objectives and what the business was about. The future story of their business was captured visually through the use of a strategy map and represented on one page.

Organically Grown Company

If you built your company organically through the CEO's own abilities and keen sense of service placement by setting up shop next to your ideal customers, having a strategy map can help you, too. With organic rapid growth you can end up going in many directions, but at some point you'll need to get clear on what your focus will be.

A strategy map helps create that clarity. There are a lot of businesses that do grow beyond their owner's capabilities. At some point you have to have that conversation with their team, the conversation where they have to acknowledge the business challenges and that something different needs to happen in order to go and grow to the next level. Again, a strategy map provides the information needed to take action.

Unite Yourselves

Diverge to Converge

The reason you create a strategic map is that it provides focus and forces clarity. Don't be surprised if this process causes your team to diverge before converging into agreement. It's normal for thinking, ideas, and documented items to initially diverge in the beginning stages of the planning process. A lot of thinking and ideas are created. Eventually decisions need to be made to create focus. This is normal part of the process.

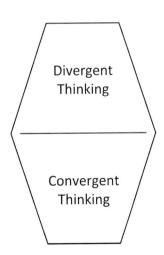

Figure 13-1: Divergent Thinking to Convergent Thinking

Eventually things will move towards convergent thinking as people start to agree on the important items and the decisions that need to be made. The strategy map is really the converging of thinking and business decision-making. This is where the business leaders make decisions around what is strategic, tactical and operational, and decide what the focus items should be for the overall success of the business.

Lots of Requirements

There are various types of requirements that come forth in the planning process. Though we've mostly been focused on strategic business requirements, planning and analysis can bring out other types of requirements as well.

One challenge I often see is the lack of understanding around the various types of requirements that a business has and the ability to link those requirements together. This concerns me, as there are a lot of leaders doing things that are in no way connected to the needs of their business and the key strategic agenda items. The **first** thing to consider is the definition of a requirement and the **second** is to know the four key requirements and how to apply them:

> A **requirement** is something that needs to be met by a stakeholder to solve a business problem or leverage an opportunity. It is a condition or a capability that is needed by the business to successfully achieve an objective. The key constraints of time, money, and resources must be addressed, and any business rules must be considered (a business rule being something that constrains the business in some way, ie. a law, contract, procedure, policy, a formal specification).[21]

There are four key types of requirements to consider when working on solving business problems or enhancing opportunities:

Business Requirements represent what the business wants to accomplish. In this case, we're talking about the goals, objectives and outcomes, the strategic agenda items, key business initiatives, high-level outcomes and buckets of work. When developing these requirements we're often utilizing the information from the business impact zones depicted in our model. The information can apply to the whole organization, a specific business area, or a key initiative.

Stakeholders Requirements represent stakeholder needs that must be met in order to achieve the business requirements and are often used to bridge the gap from the strategic to the tactical. That is from the business to the solution.

Solution Requirements are detailed and often contain specifications with an appropriate level of details to allow development and implementation They can describe solution characteristics and the environment the solution must exist in to be effective. These requirements can be divided into functional and non-functional categories (quality).

Transition Requirements are temporary requirements concerning implementation. They're needed in order to move things forward. Your people and culture impact zones will need to be considered here, especially if you are dealing with a lot of change. These requirements help you move from your present state to the future state.[22]

The thinking that goes into understanding business problems and opportunities crosses all professional and business leadership boundaries. It doesn't matter whether you're in Human Resources, Information Technology, Finance, Corporate Services or any other department. The reality is that understanding what a requirement is, gathering and capturing the right requirements, and linking those requirements together is key to creating successful business solutions.

As for the strategic planning process, your leadership team will need to decide on how best to organize your strategy map. The initial map is usually a combination of business, stakeholder, solution, transition requirements and/or a combination of strategic, tactical and operational requirements. The planning team needs to organize these requirements into their corresponding categories.

Categorizing Requirements

On the initial strategy map we cluster the business requirements into common groupings, name them, and create a statement that depicts those requirements. For categorizing there are really only three options: by stakeholder, by sequence and by purpose. You'll need to decide which method to use. Generally the decision is based on your audience and what you're trying to accomplish.

By stakeholders: clustering and organizing your requirements by stakeholder groupings.

By sequence: organizing requirements from the strategic, the tactical and the operational. This fits into the SET organizational structure and the various levels of your organization.

By requirement: including sub categories of business, stakeholder, solution (functional, quality, data), and transformation (implementation).

By purpose: generally requires that you cluster or link requirements based on their particular business process and where they fit.

In the SET-Ability model, the most common approach is by sequence (strategic, tactical and operational), as we are focused on strategic planning and analysis.

The Information Depiction

The strategic map is a matrix—a graphical display of your mission, vision and strategy—and therefore a communication tool. It makes it easy to understand and highlight your 3 to 5 strategic agenda items critical for your business's success. Because the strategy map shows linkages between the key business impact zones and the relationships between perspectives, it makes clear where the organization will have to focus and develop its resources to ensure the success of any particular objective. At this point you've clustered the information generated from the initial approach (interviews, questionnaires, assessments and workshops), integrated the information in a draft map, and categorized the formation through a vetting process with key stakeholders. And of course, all of the information is organized in accordance with the SET-Ability model.

Filled In Components

Below is a basic strategy map using the SET-Ability impact zones and linking the values, guiding principles, vision and mission and strategic agenda items to what the business must focus on. Eventually the filled in map would look something like the following.

Top 5 Core Values:	Vision and Mission:	Guiding Principles:
Service Excellence Integrity Cooperation Responsibility Well Being	To Invest in the Success of Our Clients through Providing Local Technology Support Services that are Easily Accessible to our Geographic Market	Good for Our Customers Positive Impact for Our Industry and the World Appropriate for Our People and the Organization

Strategic Agenda Items (long term goals and objectives):

A) Build a Technology Support Service company with revenue of $35 million achieving a 15% EBITDA in 5 Years
B) Engage our Corporate Culture to create the workplace of choice decreasing turnover rates by 15 % in 5 Years
C) Improve operational efficiencies resulting in reduced costs by 25 % in 5 years
D) Recognized as one of the top three support services companies in 5 years

Process and Productivity	Business Development
Build system support Infrastructure platform to improved customer experience Establish a rapid program development approach to be faster to the market Improve internal Q and A function to minimize costly errors and delays Adhere to industry best (to better) standards for service and product development	Focus on the maintenance and growing of existing customer base to increase present sales Specialize our sales force based on specific business channels that provide growth opportunities Leverage office location to improve customer and financial position and maintain market share and presence.

Tools and Technology	People and Culture
Invest in new infrastructure technology (desktop systems, portal smart devices) that allows us to be reached 24/7 Build an integrated application set for back office programs that enable improve efficiency Create a technology architect committee identify opportunities for information and data improvements	Establish an engaged and motivated workforce that has wants to be with the company through enhanced professional development opportunities Create a performance management system that links to our overall business direction Improve on-boarding approaches to ensure we have the best fit for our organizations culture

Key Performance Measurements
Revenue generations and EBITDA %, Margin by customer, $ and %, Company and department turnover rates, employee satisfaction surveys, process improvement and service level efficiencies reports, IRR and NPV realization for improvement programs, tracking customer life time value and worth over time, market penetration rates, market trends reviews

Figure 13-2: Example - Strategy Map for
Best Local Technology Support Co.

For each impact zone the company has made a statement as to what the item is and what elements make up that item. For example, under business development they have stated that "maintaining and growing existing customer base" was important to achieving their strategic agenda items. For their people and culture impact zone, they determined that they needed an "engaged and motivated workforce" to ensure their success. Each impact zone is represented and links to the overall strategic agenda items.

Layout and Format Count

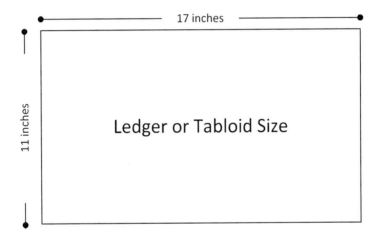

Figure 13-3: Strategy Map Size

Most companies commit to placing their strategy map on 11 x 17 inch (27.94 cm x 43.18 cm) sheets of paper (See Figure 13-3). The strategy map will contain several layers of information related to the key business impact zones -- process and productivity, tools and technology, business development and people and culture. Using a larger format allows the leadership team to see everything in one place. This makes it easier to address issues and concerns, organize strategic priorities and create agreement (See Figure 13-4).

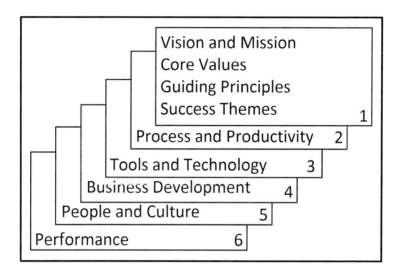

Figure 13-4: Multiple Layer Strategy Map

Often information is combined. For examples, the foundational information on page 1 (vision, mission, core values, guiding principles, success themes) may be combined with page 4 (business development) so that information is visible on the first page, page 2 might include the impact zones of process and productivity, tools and technology and people and culture. Key performance measurements may be integrated into each impact zone section. In this way you can have a customized strategic view of your company's key focus areas.

The company may also have a tactical and operational map that uses the same format.

Stakeholders See Business Requirements

One of the great benefits of the strategy map is that other stakeholders (both internal and external) can easily see where business requirements are and can then see how everything aligns with and supports the strategic objectives. This is the foundation for employee and other key stakeholder engagement. When you involve employees in growing and improving your business and provide time-proven systems for continuous improvement, your organization will experience higher levels of productivity and more innovative problem solving.

Where the World is At

Gone are the days where you could spend time creating a fancy, large, robust strategic plan that was published in some large binder or book. Today that plan would be generally obsolete before it got to the press. More and more companies are opting for the use of a strategy map format. This format provides all the elements that are part of the organization on a couple of sheets of paper (usually 11 x 17).

Imagine for a moment that you sat down at your desk or with the senior management team and everyone had fours sheets of paper with each page outlining the key strategic agenda items, business initiatives, and business impact zones against well-established measurements. What if the business requirements were front and center? What kind of conversation could you have with your team? In the event that there are external or internal changes that need to be addressed, how quickly could you address those issues and adjust your plans accordingly? Today's business world shifts too quickly to not be able to see your plans clearly and have the ability to talk about it with your team.

The Cornerstone to Future Business Success

Once you've completed an audit or assessment to benchmark where your company is at, the strategy map now becomes the convergence of all that information into one place. From here, you will know strategically, tactically and operationally what your focus areas are and what actions you need to take to optimize your business. The strategy map really becomes the business requirements.

Types of Organizations

As mentioned before, there are different ways of organizing your information. Most senior management teams choose to organize their requirements by whether it is strategic, tactical and operational. That, in turn, provides them three clear documents that outline the things they need to focus on at each level of the organization.

But regardless of how you organize your information, the strategic elements must be isolated and dealt with as key elements of your business planning. The remaining tactical and operational elements will eventually get weeded out. They can go into their own map and be secondary business artefacts. It does not mean they get ignored, however. On the contrary, they're the practical next steps to the strategic items that are going to make a difference to your business.

No Place to Hide

The overall value of a strategy map is in knowing your business requirements from a strategic perspective: there is no place to hide. Because it contains the essential lagging and leading indicators, the strategy map also becomes the centrepiece for your annual strategy review. It helps to create a business dashboard so you can monitor the health of your company--just like the dashboard in your car.

Share Them

The strategy map needs to be shared with all your key managers and business teams. They need to be fully engaged to help the business be successful. People can't help you if you don't tell them where you want to go. Share all the key elements to make sure you can be helped along your journey.

Final Thoughts

The strategy map becomes a cornerstone for the creation of your roadmap and work plans, and therefore, of your business's success. It is therefore imperative that you yourself understand the basics of having a roadmap for your business.

14

The Actionable Roadmap

An organization's ability to learn, and translate that learning into action rapidly, is the ultimate competitive advantage.
– Jack Welch

Knowing Where You Want to Go

Business leaders head out on the road everyday. Most people know what they need to get done in a day—the tasks are very operational. Take that a little farther and think in terms of what you want to or need to accomplish over a year, two years or 5-10 years. That's a bit different and requires a different way of thinking. It's more like planning a longer journey on a road with many possible destinations. In order to get to where you need to go efficiently and effectively, you need a road map.

Taking a Road Trip

There are a number of options when planning a road trip. You could, of course, just get in your car and start driving without any more than a vague idea of where you're going. You could also use a triptych provided by an external stakeholder who wants to see you have a successful trip (though whether you succeed or not has little impact on them). You would then have a roadmap that outlines various milestones and places of interest along the way. Or you could recognize that you're driving a rally car, a car that is in a race that requires forethought, planning, a good road map, a co-driver and a team with all the right skills to ensure a successful and efficient trip.

Interestingly enough, most people put more time into planning their vacations than planning for the success of their business. The reality is that, as a business leader, you need to decide what you want, the approach you are going to take, and whether you are going to drive like you're in a rally race or just meander along the road.

We All Need a Roadmap

The truth is, we all need roadmaps. Road maps help us get to where we want to go. In the S.E.T. process, it is the next step. It's the translation of your strategy map into a workable, actionable implementation plan. There can be many things tearing at the very fabric of your business that need the business leader's attention. A well-laid out roadmap can identify those things and allow you to assign a champion to take each of them on, freeing up the business leader: the driver can keep driving the road to their success.

Of course, the other option is to muddle through in spite of yourself, which is what many business leaders and project teams do. These are often folks who've built the company themselves, have created a key solution to a business problem, or see themselves as the driver and navigator in their business or project. They have a plan in their minds that no one else can see. They make course corrections on a whim. They can be unpredictable. And eventually their business can outgrow them.

Plan with Purpose

With a strategic roadmap, you can also really plan with purpose. This is not just focusing on things that need to be changed, but also recognizing what needs to be done for long-term success and tying those actions back to key strategic agenda items-- placing them on a roadmap that a well-trained rally car driver and co-driver can use to build a successful enterprise.

Keep the Car on the Road

Planning a Vacation

Imagine for a moment that you're planning a vacation road trip. Chances are, you'd consider your starting point, the end point and the return trip. You'd determine the distance needed to travel between the rest areas, refuelling, and key landmarks that you might want to visit. You might even consider the kinds of people you want to meet and the places and people you want to avoid. If you add family members to the vacation, your needs will be different: you may have to expand and change the distances to be traveled and the timelines. You would also consider a budget for the road trip, i.e. hotels, food, special events, etc. There is a cost to taking a vacation road trip with foreseen benefits, both soft and hard. The point is, you'd map out your vacation's destinations; you would have a plan to execute.

Being a Rally Car Driver

Now let's take it one step further. Imagine your business is like driving in a rally with a driver who has destinations marked all across the map, including peaks, valleys and detours. Your intention is to compete and win.

Rally car racing takes place on public and private roads with modified road-legal cars. The cars are modified just like your business. In rally driving, you don't run a circuit but a point-to-point race. There is a driver, co-driver and support team. The driver keeps the car on the road and must do so following a plan. The co-driver is the navigator. Their job is to navigate by reading off a set of pace notes to the driver. These pace notes tell the driver what lies ahead, where to turn, the severity of the turn, and what obstacles to look out for. This is important information for the driver, without which they might make a deadly mistake. So you can see, the driver must listen to the co-driver. (Though in business there might be many co-drivers.) The support team keeps the system running. Regular service and maintenance of the rally car is also key to running a successful race.

In rally car racing you can drive to win via speed, or you can achieve success through driving the journey in time stages with pre-determined checkpoints. The destination is mapped out. Once checkpoints are identified, key milestones established, the team is trained and the system is checked, it's all systems go. Some rallies are localized and are therefore reasonably short. Some are extremely long— up to 5000 to 6000 miles, like the one from the Mediterranean to South Africa. These longer races are divided into daily legs. Road rallies held on highways open to normal traffic are the original form, where the emphasis is not on outright speed but on accurate timekeeping, navigation, and on vehicle reliability. They often take place on difficult roads and over long distances. Endurance in a rally can spell success. This also applies to business.

You do not succeed in a rally without a plan. Even then, much can happen along the way that the team has no control over. The rally plan often includes the same elements that make a business successful. There is consideration for the machine: the tools and technology for success. There is consideration for the team: the people that make the success. There is consideration for the system: the process within which everything must operate and the approach to getting into the rally. Business is like a rally that the driver, co-driver and their team must take on. The way to win a rally is to have a plan.

Use a Basic Gantt

You can start the process of creating an actionable roadmap through using a Basic Gantt Chart (usually 11 x 17 inches or 27.94 cm x 43.18 cm). Your strategy map will be your key source of information and help you determine where your primary focus will be over time. An actionable roadmap hosts key information that tells your stakeholders at the strategic, tactical and operational levels what you plan to focus on and how you plan to act on it. It links back to the key business artefacts that you've already created.

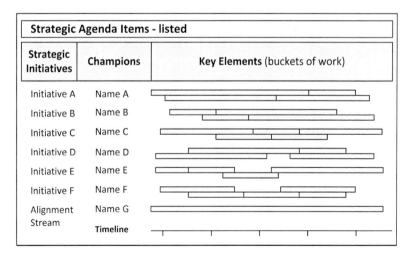

Figure 14-1: Action Roadmap Components as a Gantt Chart

When creating your actionable roadmap, make sure to revisit your business's key strategic agenda items. Your planning team should identify strategic initiatives, their corresponding business champions, key work elements, milestones and measurable outcomes. At some point an alignment path will need to be created to ensure that everything links up. The following definitions can be used to understand each element of an actionable roadmap:

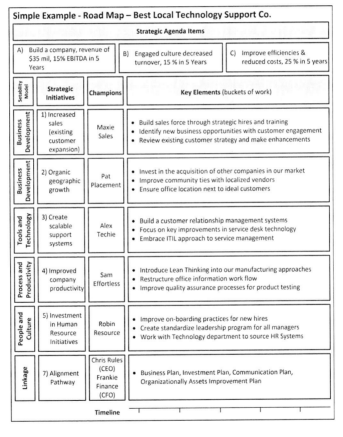

Figure 14-2: Simple Example of a Roadmap without integrated timelines and milestones.

A **Strategy Agenda Item** is a high level statement that calls for a plan of action designed to achieve the vision and mission of the organization. Generally there are 3 to 5 items on the strategic agenda of an organization.

Strategic Initiatives represent the most significant business impact zones, programs, or projects that are planned to improve your business. They are aligned with the strategic agenda items.

Champions are individuals that go beyond their operative responsibilities. As defined here, they are individuals trying to influence strategic issues larger than their own immediate operational responsibilities. They take the *initiative* and accept responsibility and accountability for it. They should bring discipline and rigor to both planning and implementation.

Measurable Outcomes are the measurable results of the implemented objectives and must be defined in measurable terms. You can pre-determine or reverse engineer measurable outcomes by using either the SMART and/or CAR principles. Always consider key stakeholders when defining measurable outcomes.

Key Elements are the big things that need to be done in order to be successful. They are the big buckets of work. The key to creating key elements is to understand the scope of work at a high level. The scope of work must be clear, accurate and complete. It also needs to be understood by a wide audience.

A **Milestone** is one of a series of numbered markers placed along a road. Within the framework of strategic planning, a *milestone* is a special event that receives special attention.

Creating an actionable roadmap can take a while. It's very common for a senior management team of 5 to 7 members to spend a full day developing a draft of this roadmap and making sure it is aligned with the items on the strategy map.

Go Where You Need to Go

The first part of creating your map is to know whether you're just driving west, taking a vacation, using a triptych or committing to a rally. The second part is to build a roadmap that will help guide you to where you need to go.

Get in Your Car and Drive

You can be successful in business in spite of yourself. In other words, you can get in your car and drive west into the frontier of the unknown, allowing everything to organically unfold in front of you while dealing with issues only as they arise. Often this turns into thriving on chaos--always needing to respond and having difficulty focusing on the long-term issues that will build on the business's success. Every corner is a new opportunity, a new adventure. Overall focus and leadership is missing.

The people working in that environment never truly know what the road is going to be like today, nor whether there will be a tomorrow. In this state, milestones are not clearly defined, and when you get an outcome, it's difficult to know if it's really what the business needs or if it's just something that happened in a hap hazardous way. The roads are littered with business leaders who just drove west.

Someone Else's Road

As mentioned before, another option is to use a triptych like those issued by your local automotive association. With a triptych, your route is mapped out for you. Someone else gives you all the key milestones and destinations. The map will come complete with your route, highlights of the route, construction areas, restaurants, and hotels. You could even get a tour book. It's a plan, but it probably isn't your plan. In some cases, external stakeholders will dictate your plans, especially if your investors or financial institutions decide you need a plan and they dictate it on their terms. In essence, they're handing you and your business a triptych, and your job is to take action on it.

Rally for Long Term Success

The last option is the one that really successful business people take. They have a plan, they have a roadmap, and they are driving in a rally. They recognize that they need a team with key navigators and maintenance and support inline to get the job done. Everyday they know they have a destination, and that destination is mapped out over a course of time with consideration for cost, productivity, performance and impact. They work with their team to be successful. Reacting when needed, but more importantly, knowing that milestones exist before a big event or outcome. If you navigate the milestone correctly in a rally, you have a greater chance of achieving the desired outcome: winning the race.

A Strategic Roadmap Helps

At some point, as the business grows and unfolds, it often becomes difficult to get the outcomes you need without the right people working with you. A road map will help you quickly see if you have the right champions on your rally team—the details that exist directly on the map.

Building on What you Know

The example map presented above is detailed and covers all the key elements that are required to ensure everything is moving forward. Everything takes time. Sometimes we feel like we have no time or we are simply impatient. A well laid out roadmap will provide the mechanism to discuss time and determine if what you need to do is possible within the timeframe required. Chances are, when taking a vacation or when planning a successful rally, you'll spread time over milestones, specific events, and distances to be travelled. In business, it's common to front load with initiatives that cannot be done in the time allotted due to three constraining resources: time, money and people. A roadmap helps you pace your rally and work successfully within your constraints.

Alignment of the business impact zones and the strategic initiatives in your business is also important. An alignment path cuts across your initiatives and the organization and is focused on the things that you need to do to make sure your business moves forward. Companies that do not define their alignment path are less likely to be successful in implementing their plans. Someone has to have an eye on that. It's no different than a rally driver whose co-driver is monitoring everything that is going on, both in the car and along the road. They make sure that things are moving as smoothly as possible and allow the driver to focus just on the road. A well thought out plan will provide you the mechanism to allow the driver to keep their focus on the road.

Fail to Plan – Plan to Fail

A failure to plan leaves so much to chance. We've all had situations where we've failed to plan and suffered the consequences. We didn't look at the road ahead. The simple example is driving to work everyday. Being creatures of routine, we take the same route everyday. What if there happened to be an accident? You may or may not make the meeting or be in the office on time. Did you plan an alternative route? In business or on the road, there are almost always alternative routes. The key is to know that they exist and having the response to these situations ready.

Underestimating Time

There are devastating results to underestimating what it will take to get a job done. Imagine you took too much for granted and assumed that the contract you've always counted on will always be there. What if you missed the RFP submission or provided wrong content due to thinking way better of yourself than you should, or employees not providing key documents on time? This could have a major impact on your business, its revenue and your people. Main business events and milestones need to be on your roadmap.

Complete Consideration

There is a good roadmap out there for your business, but it cannot be created unless foundational strategic planning work has already been done. A good roadmap considers all of the key impact zones of the SET-Ability model. This means there is crystal clear clarity of the vision and mission of the business. It also means that the leadership has made their values and guiding principles clear, and that all future decisions are based in their decision criteria. There also needs to have been a clear discussion and agreement by the senior management of what the key strategic agenda items are. Only when these criteria are met can a roadmap be developed that lays out key strategic initiatives, the business champion responsible for implementation, and the work elements required to achieve the desired results. All of this must be laid out with consideration for key milestones and outcomes and a deeper understanding of the cost, time and resources required.

Final Thoughts

Once the actionable roadmap is created, it is important that your team start the process of outlining work plans. Initially these work plans should be created at the highest levels. These initial work plans will then become the framework upon which the tactical teams will build their program and project plans.

15
The Work Plan

Failed plans should not be interpreted as a failed vision. Visions don't change, they are only refined. Plans rarely stay the same, and are scrapped or adjusted as needed. Be stubborn about the vision, but flexible with your plan.
– John C. Maxwell

Where the Rubber Meets the Road

Once you've come through the strategy map and road map, it's time to make the connection from the strategic to the tactical—to bridge the gap. This is done through making a commitment to creating high-level work plans, which then provide the detail at a level where management can take it to the tactical next steps. This is the last step towards achieving ultimate results.

Work plans provide the information your people need to know what the expectations are for moving the company forward. In addition, the high-level work plans also serve as a guide for management to deliver on work elements. Work plans help you make further business decisions. Thinking through the work plan process allows you to take a look at your three primary constraints—time, money and resources—and allocate them accordingly. This, in turn, allows your people to start moving forward on the nuts and bolts of the plans, turning your strategic planning into actual realities.

Part of this is the creation of not just work plans, but also a work matrix. The work matrix provides a visual—similar to your strategy map and your road map—that allows you to see who is responsible for what and which resources are associated with which strategic initiative. It's the bucket of work that needs to get done. With the work matrix, you can clearly see your resource allocation challenges.

High-level work plans do not need to be complicated, but they do need to be representative. The people resource element is also important here. In many ways, people resources may be your most valuable asset. Nothing gets done unless people understand what needs to be done and why it's important. It's the creation of work elements—the bucket of things to do—that the foot soldier cares about. That's where the rubber meets the road.

Failing to Develop Achievable Work-plans

Front Loading Your Plans

One of the challenges organizations face when doing strategic planning is the desire to frontload their roadmap. They put all the work up front, biting off more than they can chew. What they need to think about is time in a bottle. Think of your strategic plans over a time period, for example five years, and don't frontload everything. Lay it out in such a way that it makes sense to your business. We have limited time, money and resources, so the way in which you prioritize the work elements of your strategic plan is critical to your success.

Getting it Right

When working with a large transportation company on 26 key strategic and operational projects, the management team realized that they needed to get really clear on the initiatives linked to the strategic agenda and work elements. More importantly, they needed to identify what the activities, milestones and high-level costs would be. By putting work plans together, it helped them to understand where they would be successful and where they would have challenges. They had only 18 months to complete 26 work initiatives, each of which had bottom-line impact. The only way they would be successful was to put together work plans and a work matrix, and then negotiate for time, money, resources, and where they were going to focus. The outcome was that all the business requirements that aligned up to the strategic plan were completed two months ahead of schedule, with open testing to ensure they'd achieved the desired results.

No Work Plans at All

The opposite can also happen—a company can make the decision not to think past the strategy map and road map and fail to create work plans and a work matrix. Many companies say, "We don't have time to make plans." Once, a company I worked with in the resource industry chose to do just that. They decided to postpone building work plans that were tied back to the strategic agenda and initiatives. (Work postponed is often code for  cancelled and therefore not going to happen.) In this case, three things happened. First, the roadmap was frontloaded because there was no resource allocation planning. Second, there were no plans and therefore no accountability, so the work never got done. And third, there was no alignment focus. To this day this company is having problems due to poor business leadership and a lack of consistent focus.

Bridge the Gap

One of the main reasons to create high-level work plans and a work matrix is that, as a business, you need to understand exactly what work at the tactical level must be done in order to achieve the strategic agenda and initiatives of the organization. It's the linking of business requirements, stakeholders and the tactical or solution requirements altogether. Unfortunately, the gap between the strategic and tactical is often not bridged, and without clear direction team leads and employees will go off and do their own thing. This puts the organization at odds with itself. There needs to be a link made between what the business wants to accomplish and what the teams actually do.

Consider the Work Plan

At the strategic planning level, a work plan is high-level and might only be one page. It would carry forward items from the strategy map and the actionable roadmap. This one page work plan should include:

A **Strategic Agenda Item:** a high-level plan-of-action item designed to achieve the vision and mission of the business. These would be taken from the business artefacts.

A **Strategic Initiative:** a clear statement as to what the strategic initiative is that relates to the strategic agenda item.

An **Initiative Champion:** the person who is taking on the initiative.

A **Measurable Outcome:** a deliverable statement related to the initiative. This statement must be clearly focused on the outcome and what you need to accomplish.

Key Elements: a clear statement about the 3-5 big buckets of work that need to be done to complete the outcome for the strategic initiative. These relate directly to the strategic agenda items.

Resource Requirements: include people, time and money—both internal and external to the business.

People: a list of the people required and their roles. In this case, you can use the one of the approaches discussed earlier in the chapter about stakeholders.

The **Finances:** budget requirements and financial expenditures (if any) for the initiative.

Timelines and Milestones: detailed timelines for what needs to done by whom, and when milestones for decision-making and management reporting need to be completed.

A typical work plan has all of these elements and one should be completed for each initiative. Once that is done, work can be started on filling in the details with the people involved.

Strategic Initiative Work Plan – Best Local Technology Support Co.

Prepared by:	Robin Resource
Reviewed by:	Chris Rules and Frankie Finance
Date:	September 2014

Strategic Agenda Items	A) Build a company, revenue of $35 mil, 15% EBITDA in 5 Years
	B) Engaged culture decreased turnover, 15 % in 5 Years
Strategic Initiative	5) Investment in Human Resource Initiatives
Lead	Berti B.
Key Elements (Buckets of Work)	Create standardize leadership program for all managers
Expected Measurable Outcomes	To be assigned by the CFO and Director of Human Resources
Resource Requirements	Access to training needs research, departmental budget limits, skill gap analysis

Timelines and Milestones

Activities/Milestones	Who	When
Research leadership training programs		
Determine budget requirements		
Access government training program funding program		
Develop leadership program outlines		
Establish leadership deliverable methods (course, on-line, individual)		
Build framework and budgetary requirements		
Etc.		
Etc.		
Etc.		

Estimated Strategic Initiative Costs

High level estimate based on initial assessment

Figure 15-1: Work Plans – High Level

The Work Matrix

I came across the idea of a work matrix when I was a senior manager of global technology solutions at PricewaterhouseCoopers. I had an operational team where we shared resources on a lot of different projects. Resource allocation was a challenge, so I devised a basic table that allowed me to see where resources were assigned, where I had gaps and where I needed to cross train or cover in the event someone was not available. That work matrix has since expanded and has now become part of the SET-Ability planning process.

As you can see in Figure 15-2, information is pulled from a number of different business artifacts, including the strategy map and the actionable roadmap:

Strategic Agenda Items are the items that the senior management team stated are the high-level goals and objectives of the business.

Operational Areas include the various functional departments and their manager or lead.

Strategic Initiatives are the items from the roadmap that the senior managers agreed to focus on.

The **Champion** is the person who has taken on each strategic initiative as outlined in the chapter on creating a roadmap.

Assigned Functional Resources include any resource you've assigned to the initiative and the department they are from.

Alignment is anything that is a requirement for alignment purposes. This might include communication, education, information, etc.

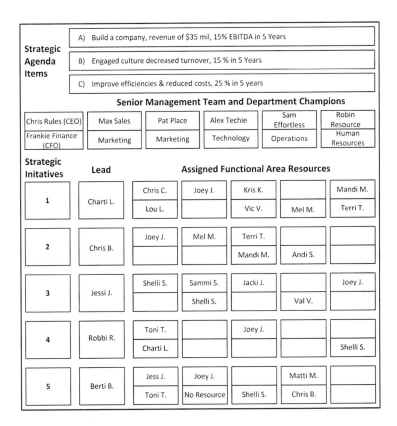

Figure 15-2: Resource Work Matrix

As you fill in the work matrix, a picture of where your people resources are allocated begins to be painted. It allows you to easily discern where you have over-allocated or under-allocated your people. It will also help you see gaps that need to be covered and holes that need to be plugged.

Rowing in the Same Direction

In the workplace sometimes people get involved in a pet project that isn't particularly connected to the overall organization. As a result, decisions get made in isolation and are not connected to the overall strategic plan. A good work plan and work matrix can avoid this, as the linkage to the strategic agenda items is made clear for everyone. They can see their part and what needs to be done. The teams start the process of working together for a common direction and end up on the same page.

At one of our retreats, a team of CEO's was asked to come up with a theme they could act out that depicted a pressing need in their companies. All 15 of them stood up, got into a boat and started rowing together. Afterwards, they were asked to explain why they chose what they did. Their response was that they needed people working together and going in the same direction to achieve the goals of their business. Everyone needed to be on the same page. Work plans help you achieve this (as long as they are followed).

Connect the Dots

Follow Through

Your people, even with good intentions, will not follow through (or will not follow through to the level you require to be successful) unless they have the guidance and support to do so. The best people to give this guidance are the business champions who were originally involved in the strategic planning. For the business champions, these high-level work plans and matrixes provide work details that connect to the overall strategic plan and roadmap. It's imperative that these business champions continually engage the middle managers and senior professionals (through consultation and feedback) to ensure that initiative's success. The purpose is to gain insight and make connections with the people responsible for getting things done. If you want to make sure you have positive business impact, engage your people in the work planning activities.

Linkage Between the Levels

The work plans for the senior people are only one page and should lead back directly to the strategic plan. They shouldn't have so many details that you can't understand them. Hopefully, your team has thought through the process thoroughly, and now the work-a-day people can understand what they need to do, allowing for accountability and an easy way to measure if things are getting done. The work plan sets the stage for status updates and dialogue, as well as for your alignment between the strategic, tactical and operational as covered in the SET-Ability model and the business impact zones. At some point detailed work plans or project plans should be created. These are best done in-house by your own people following a proven project management methodology. They know your world and they should do the detailed work. The detailed work plans and dialogue will help bridge the gap between all three business levels and can be connected into your measurement requirements, including your leading and lagging indicators. The linkage happens when your strategic goals are translated into tactical goals and work and then implemented into your business environment (i.e. becoming operational).

Final Thoughts

You may need to be guided through the process, but your people can do the work. You need to make sure the work plans are built correctly and also provide training for the people that are putting together the detailed plans so they know what they are supposed to focus on. Don't forget to also provide coaching and mentorship for the senior people who are accountable for the plans.

16

Communication Plan and Map

"Developing excellent communication skills is absolutely essential to effective leadership. The leader must be able to share knowledge and ideas to transmit a sense of urgency and enthusiasm to others. If a leader can't get a message across clearly and motivate others to act on it, then having a message doesn't even matter."
– Gilbert Amelio

It's Going to Happen One Way or Another

Believe it or not, strategic planning, creating a strategy map, building a roadmap, populating a resource matrix and creating high level work plans does not end the process. It's the beginning of something new, a plan that must be fully bought into and successfully implemented by your people. This means leadership communications.

Communication Planning

Communication planning is an important part of ensuring that the correct message is delivered and that your people are fully engaged. It's an integral part of having work done through people. How can you expect your people to act on the strategic and tactical plans unless they know what is on the strategic agenda? If your people don't know, they can't act on the plans. As a result, your business will be less likely to succeed in the execution of its strategic initiatives and tactical plans. To be successful, make sure your create, and implement a communication plan.

Give the People what they Want

Interestingly, what management thinks motivates people and what employees say is rarely the same thing. Management tends to think wages and job security are the most important factors for people, but many employees prefer inclusion, involvement, and to be appreciated for their work. This sentiment might vary depending on the working generation being reviewed, but in general people want communication. They want you to have a conversation with them, not to merely tell them what's going on and what to do. Given a lack of communication, people will invent their own ideas. As a business leader, it's important that you take the lead and make sure you're providing the right amount and right level of communication for your people.

A Communication Map

As part of the strategic planning process, the planning team needs to discuss communications from both an internal and external perspective. They need to also make sure the message is consistent. In today's world of click-of-a-button information and communication dissemination, there's no leeway for inconsistent messaging. We no longer have the luxury of writing complex communication plans. Nowadays a communication map must have the message and all channels of communication represented in a single view.

Focus on Audience

Today it's especially important to know your audience, especially considering all the possible communication channels and mediums available and the specific needs of each target audience and sub-audience. Your strategic plan's communication map should make the distinction between the internal and external stakeholders, as well as establish a connection with your stakeholders based on their communication needs.

A Multi-Lane Highway

Moving Things Forward

Having a communication plan is vital to moving your initiatives forward and for communicating your intent once your programs are approved. Remember that IT Department of an oil and gas company that had diverging departments? The company decided to have a shared service business model and bring the departments together to ensure the initiative would be successful. When we did the strategy map and roadmap, we realized that we needed to develop a strong communication plan that took into consideration all of the different levels. It needed to cut across different business units in four distinct geographic areas, as well as outline the key stakeholders, demographic needs and psychographic needs as we understood them. As a result of our analysis, we chose to use a combination of town-hall meetings, group sessions and printed communications. The program was a success. By connecting the stakeholders to the program through messaging, our people became fully engaged and that made moving forward much easier.

The Water Cooler

Proper communication from the leadership helps prevent the water cooler conversations where people fill in the gaps with what they think things mean—what they think is going on. It's important to negate negative talk and/or the unofficial communication channels where talk is misleading. People want to feel in on things. Communication is going to happen one way or another, so know what your people need and give it to them.

Finding Your Communication Vehicle

You need to identify the best communication vehicle to facilitate this happening. For example, the mining service company I mentioned previously chose an informal interview style to inform their audience of their strategic agenda and initiatives. They decided to set up an interview session with the senior management team where they'd be interviewed by a host through a question, answer and discussion format similar to that of a talk show. The topic, of course, would be the key strategic agenda items and the importance of the key initiatives. As part of this format, managers and employees could submit questions for the executives to answer. In addition, audience participation was encouraged. The interviewees were able to share about the approach they used, as well as their vision, mission, guiding principles, goals and objectives. The strategy map and roadmap were presented and each strategic agenda item, initiative and key work elements were reviewed with the business champions and their people.

This turned out to be a positive process as the employees and management felt included. They were able to provide feedback, get engaged and understand where the company was going. In fact, it was so successful that the company decided to do a road show and visit each branch office to discuss the future plans of the company. Thus, a dialogue was established.

Be Clear on Your Message

We know people are going to talk, whether it be face-to-face, by phone, email, texting, and/or the ever-expanding social media vehicles. It's just going to happen one way or another. When it comes to your strategic plan, strategy map and roadmap, you need to own the communication. It has to be handled in such a way that you can manage it—you don't want it to take on a life of its own.

Core Items to Consider

There are many items to be considered when you're looking at your communication plan and the development of a communication map. Identifying and finding the best way to communicate with your audience will be the key to your successful implementation of your plans. The communication planning process is similar to the overall planning approach— you'll still need to consider your stakeholders' wants and needs. You'll also need to find the appropriate vehicle to communicate the overall goals and objectives, the plans features, benefits and values, and find a way to address your stakeholders' questions. The following table outlines some of the common communication planning considerations.

Company Summary	Inputs: Mission, Vision, Core Values, Strategic Plan, Roadmap and Work Plans
Communications	Goals and Objectives
Situation Analysis	Financial, Demographic, Technology, Political, Social, Management, Human Resources, Physical Structure, etc.
Stakeholders Profile and Priority (audience)	Existing employees, Employees who change job status, Promotion/demotion, Part time, Full time, Term, Employees with family status changes, Family additions/deletions, Employee personal status changes, Aging workforce, Employees exiting the organization, Retirement, Termination, Employees with emergency or crisis situations, External Stakeholders, Customers, Investor, Management, etc.
Stakeholders What and Why	Communication of Feature, Benefit and Value
Communication Objective and Desired Outcomes	Actions, Time, Objective and Outcome Inform, Engage, Motivate, Maintain Desired Actions, Target Date, State Objective
Messaging	Notes on message if appropriate
Effort to Implement	Effort and Cost (where appropriate)
Communications Objectives	
Audience	Identify the various audiences
Vehicle of Communications	Announcements, Meetings, Newsletters, Email Messages, Focus groups, Bulletin Boards, Social Media, Town Hall Meetings, Webinars, Video
Frequency of Communications	Daily, Weekly, Monthly, Quarterly, Annually
Message Conveyed	Message, Value Proposition and Outcome Required
Effectiveness and Evaluation of Effort (KPI)	

Figure 16-1: Communication Plan Components to Consider

Often the importance of communications and communication planning is not well appreciated by organizations. It is something that is done quickly and with little effort in addressing the concerns and consideration of the stakeholders. When you go through your planning process, make sure you take some time to consider the communication components in the table above and work towards putting your communication needs into a detailed communication map.

The Communication Map

The communication map outlines your communication process. As part of that map, identify all of the audiences that should be involved, both internal and external. Make sure to identify what the information will be for the executive team, the managers and the operation people. Engage all your stakeholders in the process, but more importantly, identify outcomes. The communication plan mapped out gives a visual of all the approaches you wish to use to create effective communications within your organization. It helps you to manage what YOU put out there, and keep your people from looking elsewhere.

Each tier of your communication map will look differently, based upon what part of the business you're engaging. If you're communicating with your operations people, they need details of their work and what impacts them. They'll want the nuts and bolts and need to have a sense of being in the know.

If you are communicating with managers, you'll need to make sure the level of detail is appropriate to what they are managing—not more, not less. Middle managers are the intermediates and are accountable to top management, but also responsible for tactical management. As such, they will need information about expectations, timelines, budget, and overall performance.

The communication plan does not need to cover everything, however. It's more about understanding your audience, their needs, and the proper communication vehicles. It outlines your communication in one easy-to-read document, preferably in just one page. It covers your audience, vehicle of communications, frequency of communications, and it has a champion assigned to each communication requirement. If stakeholders are engaged appropriately, the value of your message will be spread by your employees. They will embrace it.

Just like the layered strategy map and the detailed roadmap, the communication plan can be represented on multiple 11 x 17 inch (27.94 cm x 43.18 cm) sheets of paper. This is especially useful in providing a one or two sheet visual of the communication plan.

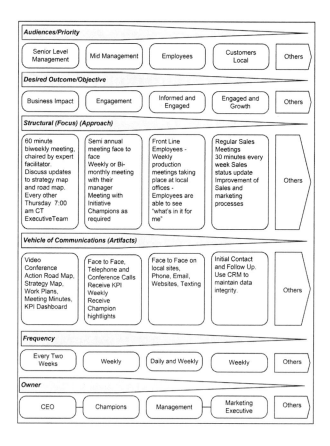

Figure 16-2: Simple Communication Plan Integrating Stakeholders and Actions to be Taken

Address Your Audience's Concerns

Be Audience Driven

To avoid speculation you'll need to create an effective communication program that is audience-driven. You need go back to your stakeholder analysis and revisit interests, goals, motivation, impact and influence. This will allow you to design a communication platform that connects with your audience— both internally and externally. There are many different communication forums to consider. The main point, though, is to make sure you address your audience's needs.

Know What You Need

There is no purpose to having a communication plan unless you know what you want to achieve. Is it high-level or are you trying to communicate with the people who are responsible for the work itself? The people who are responsible are the doers— they get stuff done. The people who are accountable is where the buck stops. These are different audiences with different information and communication needs. Another difference is that will need to consult with some people, yet only keep others informed. Make sure you're clear on who is who.

Follow a Structure

A communication plan follows a structure. It gets created only after you've put together your strategy map and roadmap. You can, however, create a communication plan before your work plans are finished. It can also be revisited regularly, perhaps as part of the regular executive meeting, once a month or every two months. Make sure you re-evaluate it after six months, however, and revisit it as part of your annual strategy review. A communication map is a living document that you need to review and keep up-to-date to ensure you are communicating appropriately in your business organization. It needs to stay alive.

Final Thoughts

We all need a communication plan in our business. It's the last piece of the puzzle. It's part of the planning and analysis cycle from the beginning to the end. More importantly, it's part of the implementation and transition process that ensures your plans get successfully implemented.

17

Go the Distance!

The price of success is hard work, dedication to the job at hand, and the determination that whether we win or lose, we have applied the best of ourselves to the task at hand.

– Vince Lombardi

What's Next?

You've gone through your planning and analysis using the S.E.T. approach. You've engaged your people and have started transitioning your business environment. The SET-Ability model has been applied and you've taken into consideration all the foundational pieces, key impact zones and measurements of success for your business. You've created your strategy map, your roadmap, work plans and a communication plan. That's a lot of work. So, why did you do it?

Was it to let it sit on some shelf collecting dust, only to be an intellectual exercise about which someone will someday say, "Hey remember when we did that strategic-plan-to-action roadmap? What happened with that?" Hopefully not. You need to go the distance, and that means implementing it. That is to say, this journey has been about preparing your senior managers, all your teams and your professionals to take your business to the next level.

Making sure the senior management team is prepared is a vital component, but it's not the only one. You need to make sure *all* of your people are prepared for the implementation of your strategic, tactical and operational plans. You need to continue to implement your plan and use it on a regular basis (as you agreed in your execution planning). You made it this far, so go the distance. Make it work. Make the investment that will keep your plan alive. Use it in your meetings, reference it, test your people on it and make adjustments as needed. No business leader or champion stops at the starting gate—they take what they've learned, agreed to, and developed, and they put it into real life practice.

Take Action to Make It Happen

Once created, the strategy map, roadmap, executive work plans, and communication plan become your key business artefacts. Now it's time to start doing the things you said you were going to do on your roadmap. It's implementation time. But what's the best way to go about it?

Put a Cycle In Place

For that you can look to a story from a company in the health care industry. One of the things they recognized on their roadmap is that, though map-sized, these plans are living, breathing documents, not just some report that sits on a shelf. The senior management team had already put a cycle in place where they would regularly complete an annual strategy review, but they found that wasn't enough. They realized that things change too fast in our world, and even if the plan is only one year old, it's already obsolete. (Don't be the organization that ignores this!) So the health care service organization placed quarterly reviews on their roadmap, as well as a review that was prior to their annual business plan and budget review date. They placed the dates on their roadmap for the next five years to ensure that it was something they could commit to.

Quarterly Reviews

Another piece that's helpful is having each business leader have a review session to ensure they are on track three months prior to any major planning session. This will keep their plans fresh, the company focused and your people engaged. By pre-scheduling in the annual review/retreat and using the core documents that you already have, you'll keep both the organization and yourself on track. In today's world, we would say that we have a GPS and it's re-calculating as you go along. In business, you need to plan in your re-calculation.

Create a Dashboard

Other information will come from your measurement dashboard (created when you discussed and agreed upon your key performance indicators). In management information systems, a **dashboard** is "an easy to read, single page, real-time document, showing a graphical presentation of the current status (snapshot) and historical trends of an organization's key performance indicators to enable instantaneous and informed decisions to be made at a glance."[23]

These days you can create a digital dashboard that will provide managers and team members the ability to monitor business impact of the various departments in your organization.

Use your key performance indicators to determine how well your organization is performing overall. They'll capture relevant data, thus providing you a snapshot of the organization.

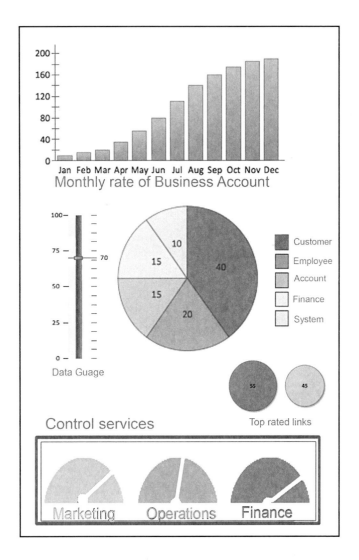

Figure 17-1: Dashboard with Key Measurements to Track Business Performance

A **dashboard**

- Offers a visual presentation of your performance and financial measures
- Collects business intelligence on the key impact zones for analyzing trends
    - o Process and Productivity
    - o Tools and Technology
    - o Business Development
    - o People and Culture
- Keeps your business aligned with the strategic agenda items and initiatives
- Ensures that your mission, vision, values and guiding principles are kept intact
- Adjusts your business's course based on business intelligence

So you see, there are many benefits to creating a dashboard for your business. Make sure you do this.

Writing CAR Stories

Every business leader and team member should be able to articulate where they are in terms of a 3-sentence CAR story (challenge, action, result). Executive-level workers should also get used to having CAR stories (challenge, action, result) for every strategic initiative and work element that they are responsible for:

Challenge: statement of the challenge they had, have or anticipate

Action: the action they took, are taking or will take to solve the challenge

Result: the result they got, will get or expect to get

If used correctly, CAR stories make it easy to provide adequate status. There's no messing around, as they're meant to be written honestly and to be straight and to the point. CAR will ensure your people are kept accountable and responsible and should be part of the business performance requirements.

Know Your Timeline

Years ago a business could do a strategic plan every five or ten years. Those days are gone. Today, three years is an eternity. Eighteen months is on the edge of obsolescence. Reviewing every twelve months keeps the strategy map fresh with the distance you've moved the stick forward in the sand, the new boundaries you crossed and the new line you created. It's all about staying at the top of your game by creating a great defence and offence. That's not done only once. You need to systematically review the playbook, your focus areas and your approach to implementing your plays.

The roadmap and the communication plans need to be executed regularly. The roadmap is a strategic artefact for the executive meetings and needs to be discussed and updated regularly. If the strategy map is your playbook, then the roadmap represents the plays to be executed. The communication plan should speak for itself—no team is successful unless they have clear communications. The business champions execute the communication plan. That will ensure the entire team is engaged, knows the direction you're heading, and are set for success.

Use a Process to Stay on Track

If you do not annually plan your retreat, you're more likely to not do what you set out to do. During the annual review, you should take a candid look at your business environment both externally and internally, using the strategy map and all the component information. You need to also go through the process of updating everything that has fallen out of date (using the SET-Ability model impact zones). Emphasis still needs to be placed on the strategic, with consideration for the tactical and operational. But remember, the business leaders are responsible for the what and the why. Let your people figure out the how, who, when and how much.

Create an Audit

As mentioned in chapter 3, audits are vital for assessing where your company currently stands, so you can make adjustments and move forward. Once you've made it through the S.E.T. approach, regular audits are a great way to have an accountability process built into your planning cycle. It needs to be on your road map and pre-booked over a course of five years, ideally before your business planning and budget period. This, in turn, will feed changes to the strategy and road maps. You can then continue to update the road map on an annual basis with strategic agenda items, strategic initiatives, business champions and key work elements over the next three to five years. From there, you update your work plans and communication plans. The accountability factors are inherent in the process: it forces you to stay accurate and on track.

Keeping Things Aligned is Key

We live in a world of rapid change and advancement. To stay on top of things, we need to revisit our wins and our challenges and set new boundaries. The executives need to re-cycle and re-check the plans. Not just the plans in motion, but also the foundational pieces of the business must be continually rechecked. This includes vision, mission, values, and guiding principles and their alignment with the strategic agenda and strategic initiatives. Maybe the world has shifted and you need to make sure that what you said you are about is still true today (or maybe it was never true). You also need to regularly recheck the strategic agenda, initiatives and the work elements to ensure that everything still aligns. If the alignment has shifted or has somehow become out of whack, it's time for a serious revisit. Remember, in today's world a lie travels at a click of a button, creating rapid and sometimes radical impact. As business leaders and champions, you'll need to ensure that you are in the game and can deliver.

The Next Level of Work Plans

Once the high-level work plans are highlighted, they need to be brought to the tactical level along with the roadmap. The senior manager and other managers need to meet to further flesh out the how, when, where and how much. The middle management needs to be involved on what is important and how often to ensure everything moves forward. All of this takes place at the status meeting level. Most companies will have a weekly tactical status meeting and the work elements need to be part of those meetings (especially if they refer to programs or projects that teams are actively working on).

Apply the Communication Plan

Make sure your entire communication plan is being applied and that all of your people are fully engaged. One way to do this is to have a quarterly town hall meeting (that would be part of your road map) so that people know where you are. Remember, people like to be in the know. The foot soldier is just as important as your team leaders, who are just as important as your senior managers, and so on. There needs to be a connection, and that connection is done through the proper channels of communication. Having the right structure for your business in place will help in that process. Actually, structure is everything when it comes to creating strategic success.

Linking Everything Together

Finally, you need to link everything together. If the strategy map is looked at annually, then looking at the road map monthly is a bare minimum. (It's actually best for it to be at the executive and business leaders' table as part of the regular agenda.) Accountability and responsibility need to be established, with a focus on the strategic (what and why) and consideration for the tactical (how, who, when, how much) and operational (here and now reality).

Establish a regular annual strategic plan review with the senior management team. For the roadmap, monthly and weekly meetings will ensure everyone is on track and will allow the champions to make any adjustments that are needed. At the project level, tactical status meetings with well-developed and implemented plans are appropriate. Use your business communications plan to stay on track.

Final Thoughts

Developing a strategic plan and an actionable road map is a journey that the business leadership needs to take. It's what provides you a deeper understanding of your business, its moving parts and the commitment needed to travel forward. Successful strategic planning leads to successful tactical and operational planning (in essence, implementation plans). Each level, as we discussed in this book, needs to be connected—the strategic, the tactical and the operational—and the only way to do that is to use a model that takes into consideration all the key impact zones of your business, as well as connecting stakeholder's needs, vision and mission, values and guiding principles and goals and objectives with the work that needs to be done.

By using the SET Approach and the SET-Ability model you can focus on your whole organization or just one impact zone and create a business roadmap that will serve as a guide to your success. If you structure your approach and engage your people, you will transform your business. You will be SET for Success.

Recommended Reading

These are books that I trust and have learned from; any one of them is an asset. You can use this list to find the ones best suited to help you learn more about being set for success in your business.

Coleman, Richard M. *The 24-hour Business: Maximizing Productivity through Round-the-clock Operations*. New York: AMACOM, 1995.

Colley, John L. *What Is Corporate Governance?* New York: McGraw-Hill, 2005.

Fisher, Roger, William Ury, and Bruce Patton. *Getting to Yes: Negotiating Agreement without Giving in*. New York, NY: Penguin Books, 1991.

Guide to the Business Process Management Common Body of Knowledge: ABPMP BPM CBOK®. Chicago, IL: Association of Business Process Management Professionals, 2009.

Hass, Kathleen B. *The Business Analyst as Strategist: Translating Business Strategies into Valuable Solutions*. Vienna, VA: Management Concepts, 2008.

Kaplan, Robert S., and David P. Norton. *Alignment: Using the Balanced Scorecard to Create Corporate Synergies*. Boston, MA: Harvard Business School Press, 2006.

Kerzner, Harold. *Project Management: A Systems Approach to Planning, Scheduling, and Controlling*. Hoboken, NJ: J. Wiley, 2006.

Kim, W. Chan., and Renée Mauborgne. *Blue Ocean Strategy: How to Create Uncontested Market Space and Make the Competition Irrelevant*. Boston, MA: Harvard Business School Press, 2005.

Lencioni, Patrick. *The Five Dysfunctions of a Team: A Leadership Fable*. San Francisco: Jossey-Bass, 2002.

Luecke, Richard. *Harvard Business Essentials: Managing Change and Transition*. Boston, MA: Harvard Business School Press, 2003.

Olsen, Erica J. *Strategic Planning Kit for Dummies*. Hoboken, NJ: Wiley, 2012.

Pande, Peter S., and Lawrence Holpp. *What Is Six Sigma?* New York: McGraw-Hill, 2002.

Parker, Glenn M. *Cross-functional Teams: Working with Allies, Enemies, and Other Strangers*. San Francisco, CA: Jossey-Bass, 1994.

Pink, Daniel H. *Drive: The Surprising Truth about What Motivates Us*. New York, NY: Riverhead Books, 2009.

Pree, Max De. *Leadership Jazz*. New York: Currency Doubleday, 1992.

Robertson, Suzanne, and James Robertson. *Mastering the Requirements Process*. Harlow: Addison-Wesley, 1999.

Rothwell, William J. *Effective Succession Planning: Ensuring Leadership Continuity and Building Talent from within*. New York: AMACOM, American Management Association, 2005.

Rumelt, Richard P. *Good Strategy, Bad Strategy: The Difference and Why It Matters*. New York: Crown Business, 2011.

Tichy, Noel M., and Eli B. Cohen. *The Leadership Engine: How Winning Companies Build Leaders at Every Level*. New York, NY: Harper Business, 1997.

Womack, James P., and Daniel T. Jones. *Lean Thinking: Banish Waste and Create Wealth in Your Corporation*. New York, NY: Simon & Schuster, 1996.

Young, Ralph Rowland. *Effective Requirements Practices*. Boston, Ma.: Addison-Wesley, 2001.

Endnotes

[1] "What Is Strategic Planning? Definition and Meaning." BusinessDictionary.com. http://www.businessdictionary.com/definition/strategic-planning.html.

[2] "TV's 60 Greatest Catchphrases." TVGuide.com. September 09, 2013. http://www.tvguide.com/news/tvs-60-greatest-catchphrases-1070102/.

[3] "Ch 1, What Is Business Analysis." In A Guide to the Business Analysis Body of Knowledge (BABOK Guide), 3. Vol. 2. Toronto: IIBA, 2009.

[4] Tenerowicz, Christina L., and Shelley S. Ruth. "Enterprise Analysis Definition." Cornnell University, 2009. https://confluence.cornell.edu/display/BAF/Enterprise Analysis.

[5] "Strategic Planning." Wikipedia. 2015. https://en.wikipedia.org/wiki/Strategic_planning.

[6] "What Is Program? Definition and Meaning." BusinessDictionary.com. http://www.businessdictionary.com/definition/program.html.

[7] Harold Kerzner (2003). Project Management: A Systems Approach to Planning, Scheduling, and Controlling (8th ed.). Wiley.

[8] "Operational Planning." Wikipedia. 2014. https://en.wikipedia.org/wiki/Operational_planning.

[9] "Stakeholder Analysis." Wikipedia. https://en.wikipedia.org/wiki/Stakeholder_analysis.

[10] "Stakeholder Analysis: Winning Support for Your Projects." Mind Tools. https://www.mindtools.com/pages/article/newPPM_07.htm. (adapted)

[11] "Our Mission and Vision | PepsiCo.eu." Our Mission and Vision | PepsiCo.eu. http://www.pepsico.eu/company/our-mission-and-vision.html.

[12] "Amazon and Our Planet." Amazon.com. https://www.facebook.com/Amazon/info?tab=page_info.

[13] "Vision, Mission & Values." RANA Respiratory Care Group. http://www.ranacaregroup.com/rana-corporate/about-us/vision-mission-values.

[14] "Vision, Mission, Values." Multicrete Systems. http://www.multicretesystems.com/vision-mission-values.

[15] Doran, G. T. (1981). "There's a S.M.A.R.T. Way to Write Management's Goals and Objectives", Management Review, Vol. 70, Issue 11, pp. 35-36.

[16] Womack, James P., and Daniel T. Jones. Lean Thinking: Banish Waste and Create Wealth in Your Corporation. New York, NY: Simon & Schuster, 1996.

[17] Persse, James R. Implementing the Capability Maturity Model. New York: John Wiley & Sons, 2001.

[18] "The Marshmallow Challenge." The Marshmallow Challenge. http://marshmallowchallenge.com/Welcome.html.

[19] Kaupapa, Tari. "Business Process Mapping." 2012. doi:10.1002/9781119198390.p 7-12

[20] "The Changing Tides of Time." Richard Lannon. http:// braveworld.ca/the-changing-tides-of-time/.

[21] *Business Analysis Body of Knowledge Guide*, 2009, pp. 5.

[22] "A Guide to the Business Analysis Body of Knowledge® (BABOK®Guide)." 2015.

[23] Wikipedia. https://en.wikipedia.org/wiki/ Dashboard_%28business%29.

About the Author

Richard Lannon

 Raised in an entrepreneur family, Richard learned to find opportunities, solve problems and implement solutions from an early age. It didn't take long for him to discover that he loved investing in the success of others. By his late twenties this had become the hallmark of all his personal and business relationships.

His cross-industry experience has made him a proven expert, one who has worked with a big four consulting firm (PricewaterhouseCoopers), top tier corporations, mid-level enterprises, and small business leaders from around the world. In 2004, Richard left the corporate world to form a BraveWorld–a company dedicated to working with business leaders and their teams to help them become successful in their businesses.

After graduating from the University of Manitoba in Sociology and Economics, his love of teaching and mentoring brought him back to the university world, where he pioneered two successful programs at Mount Royal University, Calgary, Alberta: Project Management in 1998 and Business Analysis in 2005. By 2010, he received the University's Distinguished Teaching Award for his contribution to the overwhelming success of those programs in the business community. That same year he was honoured to receive a Business Recognition Award for his work with entrepreneurs and business enterprises in strategic planning and leadership development.

Richard's research, writing and speaking revolves around what it takes to be *S.E.T. for Success* in business. In 2014, he became the voice and producer of S.E.T. for Success at 680CJOB as part of the Corus Radio Network, where he interviews business leaders on what it takes to be successful in business, career and life. He is the voice for the Tuesday Business Tips on the *All News Drive* at 680CJOB as well. His thought leadership and edgy ideas have been featured in traditional and social media, on-line publications and over the airwaves throughout the world.

As a strategist, Richard employs a unique framework to help organization's unravel complex issues, make better decisions and establish a common direction. Business author, speaker, coach, and cheerleader, Richard guides you to renewed hope, a bigger vision, and a realistic, actionable roadmap as the means to your business success.

Richard lives in Winnipeg, Manitoba, Canada with his wife, Jeannette, and their youngest son.

To inquire about working with Richard or to order copies of his book, please contact 204-899-2808 or email richard@ braveworld.ca.

www.richardlannon.ca | www.braveworld.ca | www.setforsuccess.ca